The Psychic Next Door:

Ordinary People with Extraordinary Powers

Karen Zimmerman

Stonegarden.net Publishing
http://www.stonegarden.net

Reading from a different angle.
California, USA

The Psychic Next Door: Ordinary People with Extraordinary Powers

ISBN: 1-60076-316-2

This is a work of non-fiction. Names, characters, places, incidents and images are used with express written permission.

StoneGarden.net Publishing
3851 Cottonwood Dr.
Danville, CA 94506

First StoneGarden.net Publishing paperback printing:
September 2011

First StoneGarden.net Publishing electronic printing:
September 2011

Visit StoneGarden.net Publishing on the web at
http://www.stonegarden.net.

Cover art and design by Peter Joseph Swanson

Table of Contents

Acknowledgements

This project would not have been possible without the cooperation and encouragement of its subjects – Claire Coustier, Dee Disparti, Deborah Carr Senger, Jason Lindo, Mair MacKinnon, Tiffany Vaz, and Gypse Jacquaar. Thanks for answering endless questions, and for contributing to my own personal growth. I think we all learned something new!

The publisher of my first book wasn't interested in this one because it's not ghost stories, so a big round of applause goes to Kristofer Stamp of StoneGarden.net Publishing, who loved the idea and was extremely generous with his deadline.

My editor, Vicky Walker — Thanks for your generous spirit, wit and excellent skills.

Keith Bowers, who urges me, every day, to be who I am in all my high weirdness, and vacates the house without complaint when I want to spend the whole day writing.

Introduction

Claire Coustier was the catalyst for this book, and her story begins it with chapter one.

Meeting Claire set me off on my own journey of discovery, of acceptance, and of a way of looking at the world. I was one of those kids, and adults, who people would characterize as "different." I had a lot of curiosity, and was always attracted to things that others thought were weird or forbidden.

It's the typical misfit kid type of story, but with a twist. Since I was small I could see ghosts, spirits, whatever you want to call them. I had dreams that came true. And my quest to understand what I was experiencing and feeling led me down a distinct path that was not entirely of my own choosing.

Without seeking them out, I found myself surrounded by people who were, to all appearances, quite ordinary. They had regular jobs, they grocery shopped, had car problems, good relationships or bad relationships — all those sorts of things that make up a typical life.

But they all harbored a secret, just like I did. They were constantly aware of a world beyond the everyday one. Because they had to be — they had no choice. It was just the way they were, and there was no changing it or denying it.

These people cropped up in my life in various ways. I met Claire at a local Botanica, where I was learning how to work with cowry shells as a complement to the tarot cards I already knew how to read. We became close when, after I opened a bookstore, she came to hang out and then to do readings every other Sunday.

Jason, a sensitive, came into my life when he accompanied some paranormal researchers to my haunted bookstore.

Dee, psychic extraordinaire, also she came to check out the ghosts in the bookstore. Jason, who knows Dee, suggested she might be interested in being in this book.

Mair is my massage therapist and naturopath. We met because my former massage therapist went on maternity leave. She thought Mair and I would get along well, and she was right. It just happened to turn out that Mair sees ghosts, too, and has spirit guides that help her in her healing work.

Tiffany came to me through a psychics' group on Facebook. The group has more than 1,200 members, and she was the only one who answered my solicitation for psychics to tell their story.

Deborah — so psychic — was introduced to me by Janice Oberding, my friend and fellow writer.

And then there's Gypse Jacquaar. She was the only person to answer my ad on Craigslist for a tarot card reader to work every other Sunday in my bookstore. Turns out she recognized me immediately — we had been Gypsies together in France in another lifetime. Oh, and we live three blocks apart. Go figure.

No one in this book is a "professional" psychic. They all have jobs, careers, and vocations. Psychic is just what they are, just as they are left-handed or right-handed, tall or short, thick or thin. Most do readings now and again for small sums. They seek to share what they know with others. All have kind hearts.

I conducted the interviews in person when possible, and by e-mail and phone when logistics didn't allow face-to-face meetings. Everyone answered the same questions, which led to other questions, which led to. … It all became very organic.

Besides being psychic, these people have some things in common. They share a belief in a higher power, whether they call it God or Jesus or something else. They all have struggled with acceptance in their daily lives. They've lost and made friends because of their "specialness." Their lives have brought them joy, sorrow, pain, and pleasure.

Just like you. Like ordinary people. Only these people have extraordinary powers.

Chapter 1
Claire Coustier

Claire Coustier is a library technician at the Alameda Free Library. She has worked for the Alameda library system for over 40 years, but most of the patrons don't know about her abilities.

She is a third third-generation psychic through via a vein that running runs from her grandmother, Rosa, and through her mother, Flora. Her mother's family is Portuguese, from Hawaii, and her father's ancestors are French. Her family has lived in Alameda, Calif., since 1894.

To meet Claire is to meet a vibrant, yet homey woman. She is short and, zaftig, with wavy black hair and a beautiful, welcoming face. You notice her calm, practical approach to everything and her honest desire to be helpful is what you notice. Those of us who do know her know she comes with something extra.

I met Claire at a Botanica where we were taking a class in reading cowry shells. We immediately bonded. Then, in 2004, Claire she did a reading for me. She told me, among other things, that she was sorry, but she could to see that I would lose an older male member of my family, an older member, within two years. At the time, I had an uncle who was 95, so. I figured it would be him. Everyone else in the family was healthy, I thought.

Almost two years to the day, my father died.

From 2004 to 2007, I owned a bookstore in Alameda, where I persuaded Claire to give psychic readings every other Sunday. The bookstore was haunted, and Claire she was in touch with several of the spirits there.

This is her story.

Claire Coustier's introduction to her psychic abilities came at a tender age, and in a dramatic fashion — her grandfather came back from the dead just to say goodbye to her. As we sat down to dinner, she told the story in a very matter-of-fact fashion — it was just another day in the life of a third-generation psychic.

"I have to go all the way back to when I was four years old," she begins. "My grandfather was dying, and back then, they did it the old old-fashioned way — they died at home, and I remember the whole ritual around it."

Claire recalls she was in the kitchen with her aunts, when she heard someone cry out. Her mother and grandmother, both sobbing, came out of her grandfather's bedroom with a priest. The bedroom was right next to the kitchen, where the women of the family were congregated. Soon, the men of the family came in from the yard and garage.

"It dawned on me that grandpa was in his room all alone," Claire says.

She grabbed a book, which at age four, she could not read. But she liked the pictures and she liked to make up stories about them to "read" to her grandfather.

"I went into his room, and grandfather was very still in the bed, and I can still remember how everything was set up — the sick call kit, etc., but the candles had been snuffed out and there was only one small lamp lit."

She says she remembers tugging on her grandfather's sleeve and asking him to wake up. "He opened his eyes, and he turned his head to look at me. I said, 'Grandpa, I want to read to you,' and he motioned with his left hand, over his shoulder, like this (Claire makes an over the shoulder pointing motion), and pointed to a chair — this very heavy chair that was behind me.

"I realized that he wanted me to move this chair toward the bed, because it was the only way I could climb up onto the bed. But I couldn't move the chair, as it was too big.

"So I said to him, 'I can't move it,' and from behind the chair came hands and arms, and I remember seeing a long white sleeve, and it picked up the chair and moved it toward the bed."

Claire sensed someone behind her, but she didn't look back. "My focus was to get up on that chair so I could get up on the bed and read my little book to my grandpa."

She climbed onto the bed, where her grandfather wrapped his right arm around her. She began to get very, very sleepy. And she also sensed someone sitting in the chair.

"So I says to my grandpa, 'I am really sleepy, can I sleep here with you?' I heard a voice in my head say, '"That's a very good idea, niña. Take a nap."'

So she fell asleep. "I didn't know, until a few years later, that the priest wanted to gather the family for a blessing, and they couldn't find me. They thought I might have wandered outside because the door was open."

During the search, her Claire's mother finally went into her grandfather's bedroom, and there found Claire, curled up, asleep in the her grandfather's bed, with the chair next to it. "And my mother knew that chair was not next to the bed when she left the room, and she also knew the chair was very heavy," she recalls.

Her mother, Flora, called her grandmother Rosa, who came into the room, followed by the priest. The priest took Claire into another bedroom. He had to walk through the kitchen, because that was the only way out of that bedroom, and of course, everyone asked what had happened. The priest replied, "This child has already been blessed."

Because Claire was only four, she didn't realize her experience was odd. Since she wasn't sure what had really happened, she didn't discuss it with anyone.

Eight years later, the then 12-year-old Claire, her mother, her grandmother, and her Aunt Margaret were cutting flowers and putting them into coffee cans to take to the cemetery, and they needed some twine.. Her mother dug into a cabinet to get it and came out with the twine and a children's book.

"I saw that book," Claire says, "and I said, 'Ooh, that's the book I read to grandpa!'" She had not seen the book since that night and didn't know what had happened to it. Her mother, grandmother, and aunt looked at her and asked when and where she read the book to him. She told them it was the night he died.

She pauses. "My mother and my aunt stared at me and said it could not have been, and I told them the whole story." They insisted she must be mistaken.

"No, no," they both said. But my grandmother just sat there and said, 'Wait — if niña says someone moved the chair and grandpa was awake, it's so.' And that was it. She had the final word."

Years later, when Claire was older, she asked her grandmother what she really thought about the whole event. "She told me it was the Angel of Death. And he was allowing me just a little more time to spend with my grandpa."

She continues, "If you think about it, it's scary, but the way my grandmother says it, so gently, it was just like, 'Ooh, okay.'"

I asked Claire if perhaps her grandfather wasn't really dead when she went into the room. "Well, the priest, my mother told me, had medical training, and having been at a lot of deathbeds, he knew when a person had died," she says. "No breath, no heartbeat … Grandpa was dead.

"What I think is that when the priest and my mother and my grandmother came from my grandpa's room, he had died. When I went in to see him, and tugged on his arm, the Angel of Death let him come back just one more time.

"That's scary, because here I was, doing something perfectly innocent, perfectly natural, and out of love. … And this odd thing happened. Now, when I think about it, I can talk about it and not cry about it. But for a while, it was difficult to accept."

The Angel of Death, in Christianity, is the Archangel Michael, who carries the souls of the dead to Heaven. Claire's family is Roman Catholic.

Claire Learns To Use Her Psychic Powers

Once her grandmother was aware of Claire's abilities, the training began. Rosa gave readings to everyone in the neighborhood. She would not accept payment, but people would bring her things such as something they baked or some fruit. Word got around and it was says, "Go see Rosa, she will have an answer."

Claire's first deck of "fortune-telling" cards was a gift from Rosa. They were called "Tekla Cards" and they had only pictures — no words or pips, like a regular card deck. She advised Claire to use a stone or any tiny object — perhaps a ring — from whomever she is reading for, something they might carry with them all the time, and taught her how to arrange the cards around the object. Then, "Just listen and see with your mind," was Rosa's advice.

At first, Claire didn't understand what her grandmother was talking about. "I saw her doing readings, and she talked to me about how the ability works and how at times it won't and what she would see with her ability, but I've found that with each reader it works differently and that the symbols can mean something different, never the same thing to each individual reader."

It wasn't until college that Claire started doing readings for people. One day, she recalls, "I'm sitting on a bench between classes and laying out the cards, but without anything in the middle, no object. I'm looking at the cards — they were not talking to me, but I wanted to get familiar with the symbols."

As she sat in the sun, a young man approached and who asked what she was doing. He scoffed at her "Oh, like fortune telling," he said, "That's all fake, you know."

Claire was not amused. "That's like saying my Granny was a fake." She asked him if he wanted to test the cards.

The young man agreed, and when she asked him for an object he carried with him or wore all the time, he produced a car key. A plain, ordinary car key. Claire knew this was meant as a challenge. She asked him to shuffle the cards, and while he's shuffling, to mentally push his energy into them.

"After he does all of that," Claire continues, "I laid out the cards just as my Granny showed me, around the key. Next thing I know, I'm seeing in my mind pictures and hearing voices whispering words to me and I'm telling him about this trip he has planned, but I tell him it's not going to happen and why, and about a girl he likes…"

The young man was surprised and pleased. "He asks me what career he is going into, and I see a seven-pointed star floating over his head. Now, this is 1966, and we are not going into Vietnam yet, although the war is going on, so I say that law enforcement is going to influence his career choice." It turns out that is just what the young man was considering for a career.

This young man's response to Claire's abilities stood in sharp contrast to her high school peers.

Claire's family had cautioned her, early on, to not tell anyone about her family's psychic abilities, warning that people would make fun of her. Although her family's ethnic background and culture — Portuguese and French — were accepting of psychic abilities, ghosts, and spirits, they told her, most of the people she met were not.

"I stuck with keeping things secret, until my sophomore year in high school, when it all came out. I was lucky to get a date to the prom," Claire says. "It was that bad. I didn't have friends."

It was one of those silly things, she says, where one girl kept saying of a certain boy she liked, "So-and-so is going to pin me. I'm going to get pinned. I love him so." It was typical high school stuff. But Claire knew the truth — "'No he's not! He's dating so-

and-so behind her back.' And when the girl asked how I knew that, instead of making something up, I blurted out, 'My guides told me!'"

The girl's mocking response was, "So, you're one of those. Spooky girl! Spooky girl!"

Word soon got around. Nasty letters were shoved in Claire's locker, and someone smeared feces on it on one occasion. Not one to be cowed, she got involved in drama and music, where personal differences were more accepted, but in all her other classes, she was tormented —mocked or ignored. "From then on, until I graduated, my life was miserable," she recalls. "I had no friends, nothing."

Rosa did not attempt to comfort her granddaughter. "You opened up the door," she told Claire. Rosa was not one to coddle; she was a complete pragmatist. She had warned her and Claire disregarded the warning.

She did have one classmate, Claire relates, that who seemed to accept her and was curious about her abilities. "One girl, what was her name? I can't remember. Anyway, she asked me what she thought was going to happen to certain people," Claire says. "In particular, she was interested in this one guy who was the class clown. Mostly, I was telling her, 'This person is going to do okay; this person is going to have some problems. That one is going to have five kids and no husband.' You know, that sort of thing.

"Well, she asked me about that class clown. Was his first name Rich or Doug? I can see his face right in front of me. And I looked and I looked and I told her that I didn't see any future for him. Six months after we graduated from high school, he was killed in a automobile accident."

Claire says she didn't see the boy as a spirit after he died. She told me that spirits would try to contact her, day and night, which is why her grandmother taught her about barriers. She never wanted anyone from the spirit world to come visit her in the middle of the night, so her grandmother taught her how to put a stop to that. "They were only allowed on my terms to come and talk to me," she says. "I was too young. I was a little afraid." One of the essential lessons for a psychic is how to deal with spirits when they want, not for the spirits to force themselves upon them.

Today, Claire talks to spirits all the time. Wherever she goes, if they reach out, she responds. Several of her relatives visit her at home, including one who makes coffee. The phantom coffee smells so good; it's frustrating to Claire and her boyfriend that it's not real.

Claire Meets Her Guides

I asked Claire about the spirit guide she had mentioned. "Granny explained that to me," she says. "That we each have our team of spirit guides; they come in as needed. They all have their jobs. She warned me not to confuse guides with guardian angels. You have one or you can have many guardian angels. They work on higher stuff to help us have a greater understanding and spiritual awareness, and also help you keep calm if something awful happens."

Claire went on to talk about her team of guides. "One of my guides, my alchemist, whom I call Brother John, because I didn't have a name for him, he showed himself at Mission San Gabriel, during the day. I was eleven years old."

She explains that her family went to Disneyland, and on their return trip, they stopped at some of the missions along the way, at the request of her grandmother. At Mission San Gabriel, run by a Franciscan order, they met a donkey which that would end up playing the part of catalyst in her meeting Brother John.

"The donkey had a shed, water, and feed, etc. He was easy to get to, and a very friendly little donkey," Claire remembers. "It turns out he had a job." The donkey walked a circular path that turned a wheel to pump water into the cistern so the gardens could be watered. He did it in the morning and in the evening.

"When it was his time out, he would get petted and fed. I was petting this sweet little donkey, and standing next to me was this monk," she recalls. "He had his hood up, which I thought was odd on such a hot day." The donkey turned and stretched his nose out and the monk started scratching him behind the ears.

The monk told Claire that the donkey enjoyed it. "He likes to be scratched behind the ears." When Claire offered the monk carrots to feed the donkey, "He turned to me and I remember his eyes as twinkling and blue. And he smiled. And proceeded to disappear…"

As you can imagine, Claire was a bit shocked. Her grandmother took charge. After calming her down and asking her where the monk was had been standing, Rosa walked over and began moving her hands around, as though she was feeling the air.

She turned and said, 'Ooh, that is just one of your spirit guides, not to worry,' and smiled.

Later on, when Claire meditated as her grandmother taught her, she learned that Brother John was her alchemist, and he has introduced her to her other spirit guides. "He is specifically my alchemist, and he doesn't talk to me; I just know when he is around." Claire says Brother John is the silent worker behind the action, getting her energies elevated, making sure they are flowing correctly for spirit communication.

Claire says she felt him most acutely when she was in the hospital for kidney surgery. Alchemy was a the predecessor to chemistry, and alchemists used a variety of laboratory equipment. It seemed natural that he would appear and comfort here in such a setting, almost as though he was working along with the doctors to help her get well.

Claire has seven guides, but she met them bit-by-bit, when it was time to meet them, she tells me.. She says a lot of people who are aware of having spirit guides at all think they have only one guide, but what they don't realize is that they actually have a hidden team. The guide they think is their only one is usually the gatekeeper, the one who speaks for the group.

"Another guide is my philosopher, a little tiny lady named Madame Woo," she says. Madame Woo, Claire says, is three-quarters Chinese and one-quarter English, and was killed in 1937 when Japanese soldiers invaded China. She has another who was a Navajo Shaman. Each guide has a specific function.

Besides Madame Woo and Brother John, Claire says her other guides include her gatekeeper, whom she refers to as Isis, because she has a name Claire can't pronounce. "She is Egyptian and was a priestess in one of the Temples of Isis. She prefers to work bringing in those spirits who wish to communicate and keep out those who are harmful, or warns me to take spiritual protection as needed. She doesn't like to talk through me because she does have a temper, and does not suffer fools lightly."

Her spirit doctor is Reverend Anderson, a doctor of theology and an Episcopalian minister. Claire says he died in 1918 of Spanish influenza when he was in his 60s, in Philadelphia.

She has an Indian guide, or Shaman, who is half Navajo and half Lakota. She calls him Buffalo Man, because when she sees him, he is wearing a headdress with buffalo horns. "He lived in the early 1800s," Claire says. "He is the one who tells me what I need to do if I am not well, or if someone comes to me for a reading needs to see a medical doctor.

Another set of guides Claire talks about are from not so far away — they are members of her own family.

"I have a spirit child and a spirit parent," she explains. "The spirit parent tends to rotate, but right now, it's my father's mother. That's not to say I don't have other people coming in. I will, from time to time, have other family members coming in, like my Uncle Mike. And while I wouldn't trust his business acumen, he does help sometimes, and is trying to make up for being such an SOB. Some are trying to make amends for things they did to me and to the family when they were alive."

Her spirit child is named David. "I was pregnant one time and lost the baby. But, I knew it was going to be a boy, and had he been born, I would have named him David. Now he's a grown man on the spirit side, but he's still my spirit child. He helps me keep in touch with kiddy things, helps me remain playful. He tells me it's okay to blow bubbles, to ride the merry-go-round, to be a kid."

Claire's spirit parent didn't come to her until she was a teenager. Her original spirit parent was her aunt Violet, her mother's sister. "She helped me get through my teen years and early 20s. Then, after my father's mother passed away, she stepped in."

"I kind of wondered why my grandmother, my mother's mother, Rosa, who taught me so much, didn't step in. But I realized it wasn't her job. "I even asked Madame Woo, 'How come?' I was told it isn't Rosa's job. She'll be with me when I need her. But it was not her job. She has other things she has to do. You just never know until you get to the other side what your job will be."

Claire was born in 1947, and calls herself a "twixt" child, moving between the old ways and the new. Her parents grew up with Old World culture, which played a large part in how she was raised. She says the Old World culture involved a better understanding of nature and the cycle of life, as well as a certain deportment and politeness. Family, school, and God were all-important, and family came first.

The eldest male was the leader, but in truth, in her family, Claire says, it was the women who were the mediators and overruled the men's decisions. "My grandmother was the true matriarch. The power than emanated from her was palpable." Yet, Claire has to operate in the modern world. If she had a child of her own with these abilities, she says, "I would be showing him my parents' life, my grandparents' life, and saying, — 'This is your foundation, this is where you will be learning from — this is what will help you understand all of this.'"

Three Generations of Psychic Women

It's predominantly the women in Claire's family that who have the psychic ability. Her grandmother accepted and used her abilities, and she taught Claire at her knee. And Claire's mother, Flora, had abilities of her own — she always knew who was calling on the phone and who was knocking at the door, things like that. But a traumatic experience made her turn way from her sixth sense.

Flora was born in 1919 and had three sisters. Her eldest sister, Mary, had run off and gotten married, but her two younger sisters, Alice and Violet, had died. Violet died from tuberculosis in 1937. Alice had a defective heart valve, and died in 1938.

It was Alice's death, and Flora's experience around it, that caused her to suppress her abilities. Alice had been married less than a year. Her husband, Cal, could not take care of her; he couldn't stand to see the decline of his young wife, and left her with her family. The last two weeks of Alice's' life were extremely painful, Claire told me — it was like she was having constant heart attacks. The morphine prescribed by the doctor was of no help.

Flora was exhausted from tending to her sister, so she went into the living room, next to the dining room, and sank into an oversized chair. From there, she could see through the dining room to the bedroom. As Claire tells it, "She was sitting in this big oversized chair, just exhausted. She looked up and saw, walking from the kitchen into the dining room, the spirit of her sister Violet, who had died the year before."

"My mother said she asked Violet, 'Can you make her well?' and Violet just looked at her and shook her head and walked into the bedroom. She heard Alice cry out and her mother call, 'Flora, come here,' and my mother went into the bedroom and Alice had just died. Violet had come to get her sister and take her to the spirit world."

Flora was in shock. She was so exhausted that she was in what is called a "twilight state," not quite sleeping, yet not quite awake. And this was the first time she had seen a spirit. To see her sister Violet, dead just the year, coming to get her sister Alice was just too much. So, Flora shut down her psychic ability. "My grandmother did not argue with her, understanding that my mother needed to heal in her own way."

Claire remembers Rosa as someone who knew about a lot of things. She was firm, but gentle at the same time, and very practical, Claire told me. She wasn't dramatic about anything. "It was always an acceptance of what happened and figuring out how to deal with it," she says. "I think that is pretty much how my mother and I developed. But my mother always felt she would never have the strength her mother had. It wasn't until years later that she did realize that she had it. I feel that the strength comes with age, with wisdom, with understanding things."

"My grandmother taught me by just guiding me through things, or she would see something and ask me what I was thinking. I could tell her things. I was never afraid of her. I was more afraid of my mother's discipline if I misbehaved, than I was my grandmother's. I could always tell my grandmother anything — nothing would ever faze her."

Claire shared shares a story that illustrates her grandmother's acceptance of the wonders of the psychic world, and how she learned how to accept the extraordinary.

"I was about six years old, and we were in the garden planting things. My grandmother would dig holes and I would hand her the plants. In the garden was a rose bush that grew very thick, and I heard some rustling in the bush. I looked over, thinking it was a bird, and there was this little man about 12 inches tall, maybe a little less. He was wearing clothing that looked like they were made out of bark and leaves. He was just looking at me, tilting his head to one side and then the other. He was brown, like a little nut. And I remember he had a kind of beard.

"I was a little scared, because it was like a doll had come to life. So I says, 'Bobo (that was my nickname for my grandmother) — who's that?' And she slowly turned her head and looked and says, 'Oh, that's the Menehune. Don't worry, he won't hurt you.' Menehune is a Hawaiian world for little people."

In Hawaiian mythology, the Menehune [pronounced meh-neh-HOO-neh] are said to be "little people," similar to pixies or trolls, who live in the deep forests and hidden valleys of the Hawaiian Islands, far from the eyes of normal humans. It's said they have lived in Hawaii before settlers arrived from Polynesia many centuries ago. They can be up to two feet high, but some are so small, they can fit in the palm of a hand. Often, when they are seen, they run to the shelter of the forest.

Legends say the Menehune enjoy dancing, singing, and archery. They have been known to use magic arrows to pierce the heart of angry people to ignite feelings of love instead. Furthermore, their spirits are always changing; one could be malicious and dangerous one day, and harmless the next. They are described as cunning creatures, and should be avoided, unless you need a special favor from them.

"The Menehune are very protective of certain trees they would consider sacred or as their homes," Claire says.

I asked Claire why she thought this creature was in her yard and why she was allowed able to see him.

"Maybe because I was working with my grandmother and we were planting things. My grandmother always saw the garden as a sacred space. Nothing is cut, nothing is removed, until she asks permission, and she gives an offering, whatever it might be. In this case, he deliberately wanted himself to be seen for possibly two reasons. One, to let me know that there are little people and to let my grandmother know, so that she could see he had taken up residency in her garden."

"Because, after that, my grandmother went out and bought a special doll-size tea set. And every Sunday, she would take a little bit of the food from dinner and mash things up; make it easy for a very small mouth to eat." Claire would take the food and place it near the rose bush. She would do that every Sunday, and every Monday evening, she would get the dishes and everything would be empty.

"I would bring the dishes in and grandmother would wash them. So, this little Menehune had Sunday supper," she says, laughing. "I remember that summer, the garden, the vegetables. Everything grew wonderfully," a sign that the Menehune was taking care of the garden.

Rosa died in 1971, when Claire was 30 years old. After that, Claire's Uncle Manny kept up the garden and the Sunday supper ritual until he died in 1977. The house was to be sold, so Claire visited the rose bush one last time.

"When we were clearing things out in the house, I found the tea set and made one last Sunday supper. I put it out and says 'Menehune, this is going to be the last Sunday supper. My grandmother has died and my uncle has died, and the house is to be sold, so you'll have to find another place to stay.'"

She went back on Monday evening and washed the empty dishes as usual.

Within a week, everything in the garden started to wilt and wither. "And my mom said to me, which I thought was a little strange, because I didn't know she knew about it, 'Did you tell the Menehune the house was sold?' and I said yes. And she says, 'Okay, well that explains this, because everything was just blooming and green and then we saw leaves dropping and everything dying the last two weeks we were there.'"

But, it isn't only the women of the family who have extraordinary experiences.

The Men of the Family Share the Gift

For some of the men in on Claire's mother's side of the family, psychic ability took on a different cast. When Uncle Manny, held a piece of wood, it was like he was communing with the wood, she says. He somehow knew what it wanted to be, and he would build it. He was the same way in the garden, where he had a green thumb.

Her Uncle Henry had an odd experience in World War II that shaped his faith ever after. "He was a sharpshooter stationed in Italy," Claire says. "What they called then a point man, which nowadays would be called a sniper.

"That meant he had to go out way ahead, find a spot where he couldn't be seen, and radio back what he saw," Claire says. "And if there was the enemy approaching, it was his job to take them out, especially if it was an enemy sharpshooter."

Henry holed up in the bell tower of a church, choosing that spot because there were no civilians or animals around. "So, he was up in this church, in the bell tower. And what happened is that evidently, the German sniper was probably a little bit better than he was, or Henry made a clumsy mistake — and he got shot. The shot knocked him out of the tower, and he rolled down the roof of the church. Telling the story later, he recalled his last conscious thought was, "Okay, I'm going to hit the ground, break my back, and I'm going to be dead."

It wasn't until he was recovering in the hospital that some of the buddies in his unit told him what had happened. Apparently, when he rolled down the roof, he fell into a wagon filled with hay that had with a horse hitched to it. "He landed in the cart and the horse took him back to his unit," Claire says. "The cart had no driver. It just came to the unit headquarters, and the men stopped the horse. It had gotten close to the hospital and they didn't know how it had gotten that far without being stopped by sentries.

"They found my uncle in the back, took him out of the wagon, then turned around to the wagon and horse — and they were gone." Henry knew there had been nobody around when he chose the bell tower. Now, my uncle knew quite clearly that when he went into that bell tower, he chose that spot because there were no civilians around, no carts, no animals. They had all been moved out.

"That cart should not have been there.

"The incident gave him a chance to get some R&R. He went to the Vatican and talked to a priest and told him, 'I'm a sniper, I have to kill people,' and told him about the incident with the roof, cart, and horse. He must have gotten hold of a good priest, because he helped Henry come to a peaceful resolution about his job. The priest says, 'If God hated you, that cart would not have been there. So, it was meant to be, and God forgives you, even if you have to do something as ugly as that. God is letting you know he forgives you and he loves you.' So, he had his own special experience."

Her father, Bert, also had an experience— he saw the ghost of a dead nun when he was a boy. "And, he would get a sense of things," Claire says. "He was very accepting of mom and my grandmother and eventually, me, of our having this ability."

Life in a Psychic Family

Claire continues with more stories of her family's psychic prowess

"One time, my grandmother was sitting on the porch with me and our neighbor, Mrs. Byrd. A card drove by and my grandmother says, 'He is going to kill his wife.' Just like that. And it wasn't even her voice. I was a terribly different voice. I never heard her speak like that. She always spoke with an accent. This voice had no accent – I don't know who it was."

Such was Rosa's reputation that Mrs. Byrd told Claire to stay with her grandmother and ran into the house to call her husband. "Next thing we know, Mr. Byrd is running like mad down the street to another house. He arrived just in time to keep the man from murdering his wife."

Claire says her grandmother went into a somewhat of a trance. The same thing happened to her mother sometimes. She recalls one instance when her parents were in the car and a motorcyclist sped past them.

"A similar thing happened with my mother," Claire continues. "She was with my father in the car and a motorcyclist flew by them. My mother says, in this odd voice, 'Go, go kill yourself.' And a bit up ahead, the motorcyclist did crash and was killed."

It happens to Claire, too, but not too often — which she's happy about, because it freaks out her longtime boyfriend, David. She describes it as a semi-trance. She's aware of where she is, but everything looks different.

Claire and David have been together since 1993. She has told me about high school, but what of friends and romance before she met David? Claire says that she isn't always so psychic when it comes to her own life.

"I didn't date all that much," she says. "Word got around about me, you know — Alameda in many ways is a small town. And so, the guys I dated weren't all that high on the food chain, if you know what I mean — not really boyfriend material."

She was married once, to Lloyd. "If two people should not have married each other, it was Lloyd and me," she says. "I was 20 and I was feeling pressure, especially from my older peers at work, and my mother and dad were worried. It was hard to find a guy who I felt was my financial equal, with a good job, and no kids."

She wondered why her guides had not tried to talk her out of marrying Lloyd. She says she realized later, when she asked her gatekeeper Madame Woo, that her early marriage was something she had to go through and learn from, for her own personal growth. It lasted two years.

She did get engaged again, to Bud, at age 35, but behind her back, he married another woman.

Claire sees these failed romances as learning experiences. "I had to go through those two relationships to understand relationships, to be able to help other people. Similarly, she says losing her child helped her too. "The fact that I did get pregnant, and lost the child, helped to figure out if I had what it takes to be a mother and I discovered that I did not have that," she says.

"In a way, things worked out. I ended up being a caregiver for my mother, and if I hadn't been her caregiver, she would have ended up in a convalescent hospital, which I would have felt so guilty about, it probably would have preyed on me the rest of my days." And, life experience adds up to life wisdom, which helps her in her psychic work.

As for friends, her current friends know who she is and about her special abilities. But what about co-workers — and do her abilities affect her job?

Claire responds with a laugh. "Not really. Let's put it this way —— it took years before I would even allow myself to be 'out' with my co-workers." They didn't know she was psychic, but they knew there was something different about Claire — she had a lot of arcane knowledge about tarot, palmistry, the paranormal, and the occult. In the case of one library patron, this proved fortuitous.

"The reference librarian got a call about tarot cards. Because I was the person who knew 'weird stuff,' the call got transferred to me. I talked to the person and asked them to come in over my lunch hour.

The patron was a frightened teenage girl. She and her friend had been reading tarot cards. "The friend pointed to the death card and says, 'You are going to kill your parents.'" The girl was really scared, because she thought it was going to come true." Claire was able to reassure her. "I was able to let her know that the death card just means change — it was about her growing up. The little girl is gone and the young woman is coming into place, and given the surrounding cards, it was hard for her parents to accept this."

Claire says it wasn't until her current boss arrived that she felt really accepted. "We actually talked the other night about exorcising the current library," she says. "He's convinced the building is haunted. We'd had strange things happen the last few weeks. It started just before we had an earthquake close by, and then these electrical storms," both of which, she says, can release spirit energy. "He came to me and says we had to exorcise the place.

"I asked him if it was because someone (a spirit) was bugging him in his office. He wanted to know how I knew that!"

Claire explained that she often sees spirits walking around the library. "The library is built on the site of an old hotel," she says. " I know there were at least a couple of suicides, some ODs, bodies had been found there, etc. And, before WWII, this is where the Chinese and Japanese communities resided. There were houses here."

She has done readings for her boss's wife, and he doesn't mind when she occasionally gives readings in the library's café. Sometimes she uses cards, sometimes an object; sometimes she just holds someone's hand.

For a few years, Claire gave readings every other Sunday in my bookstore. She feels the responsibilities of doing readings keenly. "I like when I can give positive feedback about what someone is doing," she says. "Telling people negative news is another thing altogether. I try to give things a positive spin. Sometimes, people can change things that are going to happen. Sometimes, there's no help for it.

"In one case, I did see a car accident approaching a woman, and I didn't want her to be frightened about it. I told her my guides wanted me to give her a warning, and that she had the power to change things. I told her she needed to check out her vehicle, and told her if she didn't, she would have a big problem. If she did have it checked out, the accident will still happen, but it won't be as bad." The woman got her car checked out, and called Claire to tell her that what she predicted did indeed happen.

I got some feedback from another of Claire's clients regarding a more mundane matter — wood rot in her house. "Claire told me exactly where my contractor was going to find the rot – it was incredibly accurate," the woman told me.

She tries to turn a reading around from a negative to a positive — it gives people a more hopeful mindset. "It's like the girl and the tarot reading," she says. "It's how you approach it. I never, ever predict death. I never say that someone is going to die, unless it's someone I know very well. But, sometimes, I have to prepare them for something bad and give some guidance."

Some people, she cannot read for at all, she says, and it's usually because they have put up psychic "walls" to try to keep her from finding out about their lives. "I remember doing a reading for one woman. I could get things about her son, but she kept denying it and I told her to just file it away, because my guides will not let go of it. But, trying to do a reading for her was all but impossible. I kept seeing these opaque glass bricks that were covered with dark slime and fungus. I simply could not see her at all. I felt bad and told her I would not take her money."

Several weeks later, Claire ran into the woman at the supermarket. The woman apologized and told Claire that a number of things she had mentioned about her son were correct, but she didn't hadn't known that until she had a chance to talk to him, and hadn't wanted to believe them at the time. The woman also told her that what Claire she saw was accurate, in a way, since she has had Lupus, but she didn't want to discuss it — the bricks with the slime symbolized her illness.

Sometimes, people try to trick Claire. Once, she was doing readings at a party. "I was giving a demonstration of psychometric ability," she says. Psychometry is the ability to psychically read an object and make associations with someone's life.

"The daughter of the hostess deliberately tried to trip me up and gave me an earring she had borrowed that very evening before the party from a friend of hers, who also was at the party. So, I as giving the reading, she kept saying, 'No, no, that's not right.' Finally, I looked at her and something had me say, "Well, of course it's not right for you, because it feels like these are not your earrings.' Her friend's mouth dropped open and she says, 'those are really my earrings, and everything you said was right.'"

Other Influences

I asked Claire where, besides from her grandmother, she got her vast body of knowledge about the psychic and occult. "Through the ladies of my Granny's group," she says. "They would find someone who could come over and give a talk about something dealing with the paranormal — one of them was a Satanist long before Anton LaVey was any kind of household word, and thanks to him I learned how to not be open, how to protect myself, and how to recognize hidden evil. Not that he did anything bad to me — he didn't, but he explained what evil was and is, and how easy it is to control people, how easy it is to manipulate them. I won't mention his name because I think there are some of his family members still alive." Claire also had a much older cousin who was a nun; they exchanged long letters.

She even met psychic Sylvia Browne. "That was a very interesting, if altogether too brief meeting," she recalls. "She brought in a friend of mine who had passed over — got his name, and even described his tattoos. She says that eventually I'll write my own book, but I'll be afraid to publish it. I think she's right; I just don't have the drive to pursue getting a book published. And writing one? I wouldn't know where to start."

"Now about books. What haven't I read? In ghost hunting I'd have to credit Hans Holzer of course." She also was influenced by the famous witch Sybil Leek, "But as I look back on her works, they seem so naive, like she was still holding back things." And, works by Sylvia Browne, because, "What she describes comes very close to what I've experienced as well. But if there's any one work that just struck me as having a serious influence, I'd have to say *Ghost Hunter* by Hans Holzer — if anything he confirmed and re-affirmed that all the psychic experiences that I've gone through were real and not imagination; that there really is a spirit world out there."

But what about everyone else — can anyone develop psychic powers? Claire is doubtful. She believes it is something you are born with; you have abilities of one sort or another or none at all. "There are some people who have abilities as healers. So, if they are in the medical profession, they are using their ability. There are other people who are the dog whisperers. And there are people who make others feel very, very good. They are mood elevators. And, there are empaths, who can channel and dissect the emotions of others."

People use many methods for doing readings — it's all like some sort of radio to help elevate the harmonics, Claire says, and tune things in. And objects like Ouija boards are not inherently evil, despite popular belief. They hold no innate power in any of these things — it's all about intent.

"It's the person handling these things," Claire says. "You get a bunch of teenagers playing around with a Ouija board, you have to stop and think of all that poltergeist energy they are releasing," she says. "It's like that book, *Conjuring Up Philip (An Adventure in Psychokinesis)*, where a group of kids got together and literally conjured up a spirit via their collective consciousness. And that's what they are doing – they are releasing all this energy and they are creating those spirits.

"You are courting a problem. And then they say (in the book) they called up demons, etc., and they are feeding it with their fear. In that case, they need to get rid of the board and allow that energy to dissipate — it is a creation of their fear."

Claire feels her abilities came from God. "I'm using 'God' as a generic term. I was given these abilities, I was giving given the responsibility of them, and I accept that and I try to use them for the greatest good.

"But, I have to protect myself, too. If I didn't, I wouldn't be doing readings for people."

Claire doesn't do a lot many readings these days, because she has to have a place where she can feel safe and mentally set up a sacred space. She does this by centering herself and praying to keep out negative entities and influences. During a reading, she says she calls her guides in and tells them "We've got an appointment," and they will tell her they are present. She doesn't advertise, and so those seeking readings are usually people who have heard about her from a friend.

She isn't sure how much longer she'll be giving readings. "I am aware that as I get older and develop illnesses that, in time, my abilities will diminish. When and how that will happen I don't know," she says. "My Granny used to say that '...As one begins to get older, one wants to be more with the living than with the dead. And then there comes a time when the dead become the few visitors that you have, when you get closer to the other side, only you're not aware of it because it's like a dream, a dream that you want to live in forever.'"

Those interested in a reading from Claire should email ccoustier@yahoo.com.

Chapter 2
Tiffany Burch-Vaz

Not all tarot readers are psychic. Some are great interpreters of symbols and have an affinity for the cards. But, there are others who have abilities beyond mere interpretation, who "see" future events along the seeker's current path. This was the type of person I was interested in for this book. I knew several and I had some referrals, but wanted more subjects.

I met Tiffany through a Facebook psychic's group. On the surface, we couldn't be more different. She's a stay-at-home mom of four in the South, soon to be moving to Portugal. I'm a single woman living with my boyfriend and two lovely cats in the San Francisco Bay Area, and go to an off-site job every day. But through our email correspondence and question upon answer upon question, we found those common threads that weave us all together, further proof that psychics aren't that much different from me. Or you.

Tiffany is from Georgia, but currently lives in Portugal.

Tiffany Burch-Vaz is an unlikely psychic from an unlikely state — Georgia. A little research tells me that the predominant religion there is Baptist, the members of which share a belief that the only ghosts are either angels or demons. Her family was no exception.

Her mother and grandmother both had experiences, Tiffany learned, but calling them psychic made it seem dirty in the religious household. "It took a while to convince my parents, after I dropped the 'psychic bomb,' that I was not working for the Devil!"

When her father became a born-again Christian a few years ago, he decided she had become a Devil worshiper and suggested she get back to church. Luckily, she spent a summer with a psychic some time earlier, who warned her about this sort of family reaction, because it had happened to her.

"She showed me a quote from the Bible to use when someone starts to speak of how 'evil' this is, and that I needed to be saved," Tiffany relates. "I think they have finally started to come to accept the idea of me being psychic, or at least having abilities out of the norm and turning it into my career outside of being a stay-at-home mom; but I do not think they would ever announce it to their friends or members of their church. If someone should ask them about my abilities, I don't think they would acknowledge them, either for fear of being labeled, or rejected by their church and community.

"It really is disappointing when someone hears a term and automatically puts you into some imaginary group, and more so when it's your own family," Tiffany says. She understands that this happens because it is what they have been taught to believe, either through their religious belief system, or through the stereotype society has of psychics. She thinks that people are reacting out of fear, since much of society really does not understand what psychics do. And, in her experience, few people ask about her gift with an open mind. Much of what psychics do cannot be seen or scientifically proven — or at least not enough for many skeptics. She wonders how many truly believe in a God source, too. "Think about it: If you really believe in a God, then you have to believe in things that you cannot physically see or even prove," she says.

"My first thought was, if my own family was thinking these thoughts, then what would other people say and do? I felt that if I could not convince my own family that this was not some dark and evil thing then I had no chance of ever convincing other people."

Tiffany believes that her powers come from God. She believes in a universal God. "A God for everyone; that, not only if you believe a certain way can you have access to this God, but a God that loves every single one of us no matter what we believe or practice as our religion."

Tiffany was raised in Macon, Georgia, and was exposed to the Baptist faith, but her family did not attend church when she was growing up. In her early twenties, she became interested in Catholicism, but was wary of visiting a church alone because she had been told that "Catholics worshiped statues and were all drunks."

She met her husband Tony, a non-practicing Catholic who had been visiting Baptist churches in the area. Tiffany still wanted to experience the Catholic faith, so they eventually started going to Mass together and she joined the Catholic Church in 2005.

Despite familial disapproval, Tiffany's psychic abilities grew as time went on. She tells me that she feels God wanted her to explore her abilities as a way to help people. And so she backed away from the church in order to pursue further psychic development. She joined a Spiritualist group, but didn't feel like she belonged there, either.

She feels she doesn't fit into just one belief system, because she thinks we should not limit ourselves by feeling pressured to select only one path to God. Today, she belongs to no particular religion. She believes in the principle of karma, and says she tries to love and respect everyone.

Learning she was psychic

Tiffany's first psychic experience happened when she was only two and a half years old. She has no memory of it, but it has become a family legend. "My grandfather became ill and was admitted into the hospital," she recalls. "He was not so ill that the family was expecting him to die at this time; this was just a routine trip to the hospital for an elderly person. Because I was so young, I was not allowed to visit, but my uncle decided he would sneak me into the hospital.

"While we were visiting, and my grandfather was sharing his ice cream with me, I announced to everyone that Papa was going to die. Apparently, this stunned my mother and she was trying to recall if anyone had mentioned this possibility to me, but since no one admitted they had said any such thing, the subject was dropped. Keep in mind that no one was thinking this would be anywhere near the last days of his life. Sadly, about three days later, my grandfather did pass away."

Tiffany's next experience came at age five, when she looked out of her bedroom window and saw a little girl looking back at her. She was frightened, and for a long time, she didn't like to look out of that window. Tiffany remembered that the girl was not wearing modern clothing, but looked like someone from the television show *Little House on the Prairie*. Around this time, Tiffany says she would clearly hear someone in the house calling her name. She thought it was her mother, but after asking, found it was not. It was a woman's voice, but whose it was remains a mystery — she and her mother were the only ones home at the time.

While some psychics have rapid-fire experiences and their abilities seem to bloom in an instant, others have a string of randomly spaced events that culminate in a deeper understanding and realization of what is happening to them.

"We moved from that house, and I cannot remember much happening until I was 10 years old," Tiffany says. "My grandmother had a very old Chihuahua named Poncho that had passed over several years before. I do not think this dog liked me much, since he was old and I was very young and always wanted to play with him. He always growled at me and I cannot remember a time when he actually enjoyed my company. Several years had passed, and we had since moved to our new home, which my parents built. One night I awoke to see Poncho sitting in my room next to my bed. I remember looking at him and blinking and thinking he is no longer living, but here he is looking at me. I decided to call out to him and he disappeared before my eyes."

She told her mother and grandmother about her visit from Poncho, and for the first time, she learned that both women also had seen spirits. "We have always, from that time onward, spoken freely about any dreams, and premonitions we had, or spirits that we experienced."

Her mother and grandmother did not seem to fear the ghosts they saw, which Tiffany says were full body apparitions. Thinking her grandmother might be teasing her, she asked her again and again about her experiences, but her stories were always the same. Her mother also always told the same stories. Over the years, as the three women would talk of these experiences, "they just seemed normal to me until it came up in a conversation with someone else, and I would see their reaction," Tiffany says. "This is when I realized that not everyone has seen a spirit."

Her mother and grandmother were not the only family members to dabble in the other side. Tiffany's great-aunt, her grandmother's sister, held "dumb suppers" that were rarely discussed.

"From what I can understand, my aunt would cook a meal for the dead or in her case a daughter and husband that had passed away," Tiffany says. "The meal was prepared in a certain way and you could not speak while preparing or eating the meal, and places were set at the table for the 'guests.' I heard from family members that these dinners did bring about spirits."

My own reference for the dumb supper was a short story by science fiction writer Kris Ottman Neville, writing under the pseudonym Henderson Starke. Teenage girls hold a dumb supper to find out which boy one of them will marry. One girl cooks a meal, with all the ingredients added in backward order, stirred with the opposite hand usually used, all walking backward. Two places were set — one for the girl, and one for her phantom groom.

All is done in complete silence. Wait…wait…and at midnight...

The dumb supper is an old pagan tradition, tweaked to fit the purposes of the participants. The short story illustrates what can happen when rituals are used in a frivolous manner. Most who hold a dumb supper hold it in reverence of the dead, hoping for a short visit in a homey setting.

Given this family story, Tiffany thinks this is why it was not so strange to talk about spirits — experiences with them ran in the family. "I was also told that my great-grandmother would visit psychics, including a very well-known psychic that would travel about during that time, which would have been around and before the 1950s. My grandmother also mentioned on several occasions sensing my grandfather and smelling his cologne in the kitchen years after he had passed."

While her grandmother gave her little guidance in using her abilities, she was supportive and never treated Tiffany as though she were odd, or as though she just had a vivid imagination. Tiffany says her mother is more of an observer. She likes to hear what the family has experienced, but she thinks her mother fears being teased by others. "I will share my experiences with her, but not in the way of looking for guidance. I think with grandma, our conversations on this subject seem more equal and we can talk and explore the idea of spirits."

Psychic Development

Tiffany's psychic experiences seemed to slow down as she matured, she says, happening intermittently during her teen and young adult years. When she started having children in her late twenties, her sixth sense became more active.

"I have thought about this often — why did I have those experiences and then nothing much? The only thing that comes to mind is that somehow I rejected my abilities."

She heard about the psychic world from a classmate who read tarot at their Christian-based private high school. She also was brought by a friend to a roadside psychic for a reading, but neither experience piqued her interest or made her think about what she had experienced with spirits previously, or about her abilities.

"I think these might have been tests for me to determine if I was ready to take the journey or not. I don't think I ever realized that people actually prepare for this by working with a teacher or through reading books. I guess too, that at that time in my life I was more interested in being popular and pretty and most of all — having fun!"

Tiffany says that after she was married and became more involved in church, she was less restless. She began thinking about her spiritual side. "I was open to learning about God, and curious about how my life was going to be different with having children. I think the fact that I had become 'open' was key."

At the time of the 9/11 attacks, she had two small children, and was active in a moms' group at her church. She remembers feeling a few days before that something awful was going to happen, and told a couple of friends in the group, explaining how she experienced a "huge feeling of sorrow," but did not know why. They simply told her to stop thinking like that, rather than being interested in her feelings and what they might mean. Afterward, she says, she started to see the group differently, wondering how she would continue to fit in with them, and recognizing that she was a little different from other people. She also started to reexamine her belief system and to reconnect with her gifts.

Her Specific Abilities

Tiffany says her abilities include being empathic, clairsentient, clairvoyant, clairaudient, and mediumistic.

She explains her powers thusly: "Empathy is the ability to tune in intuitively or psychically to the moods and characteristics of a person, animal, or thing. This is one that I have always known from a young child. I just seem to know the moods of people, and also if someone didn't like me very much. I also seem to draw people to me who wanted to share personal information, such as sexual abuse that they had experienced as a child. This occurred several times — and since I was NOT a child of sexual abuse — I just thought of myself as a 'cosmic garbage can' where people could dump their problems and I would see that it disappeared into a 'cosmic dump.' It always seemed to make each person feel somewhat healed once they told me of their abuse.

"Mediums serve as a channel for communication between the living and the dead. My first experience would probably be that little girl in the window, but I would rather count Poncho, my grandmother's dog. I later had a dream of meeting an Aunt Nora. I asked my grandmother if I had an Aunt Nora. She told me that I did, but when I asked to meet her, she told me that Aunt Nora was no longer alive and had been dead for many, many years. As the years progressed, I was able to communicate with the spirits, but I do not claim this to be one of my strongest abilities.

"Clairaudience is the ability to receive psychic impressions of sounds, music, and voices that are not audible to normal hearing. I was in my early twenties when I had a mole removed. I wasn't so worried about it until I heard a voice (in my mind) plainly tell me it was cancer. It came back to be malignant melanoma.

"Clairvoyance is known as 'clear seeing,' and refers to the ability to see an event or image in the past, present, or future. This first happened while in high school and seemed a little like déjà vu at first but I remember seeing a guy who was my boyfriend at the time, and someone that I really liked, meeting up with a friend of mine at a party. It later happened the way I saw it in my mind."

Like Claire, Tiffany has spirit guides who help her with her work. Her newest is Father Samuel. "It was very interesting meeting him," she says. "My husband and I were in Florida and we were walking together. We started talking about religion and God, when out of the corner of my eye I see a Franciscan monk walking next to me, wanting to join in on the conversation!

"I have another guide that I call Inara, and she is from somewhere else that I cannot pronounce but she is a purple mass with sparkles, kind of in an S formation. I also have a Native American woman guide named White Feather, and each time I see her she has more and more white feathers in a basket and in her hairpiece. I think the feathers represent the people I have helped, because when I first met her, she only had one white feather.

"I have a guardian angel, Ariel, and she seems to be more of a protector, along with Sabra, who is my animal spirit guide, and is a saber-toothed tiger. I also have noticed my cat, Maggie, who passed away two years ago, around Sabra. They seem to hang out together, which is funny and odd, but since Maggie has been around so much, I guess she is in the group, too."

Tarot

Tiffany told me that she bought her first deck of tarot cards in 1994. She ordered the Mythic Tarot from the back of a magazine. "I felt compelled to order these cards, and so I did. I knew nothing about tarot at the time."

The Mythic Tarot offers an imaginative approach to classic Tarot. Each suit depicts archetypal characters from Greek mythology, and every card tells a story about that character. These mythical legends illustrate wisdom and insight for personal growth.

Tiffany says she has owned other decks, including the Rider-Waite, Thoth, and Morgan-Greer, but gave them away because they just did not "speak" to her.

"I sometimes will use my Osho Zen tarot deck — this deck drew me in after I saw the cards at a metaphysical store. I just could not stop thinking about them, and so I had to have them. But, it took me about a month of thinking about them before I finally did buy them!"

She will occasionally use an angel or oracle card to bring clarity to a reading, but sticks with her two favorites. "It sounds strange, but sometimes my Mythic Tarot cards do not want me to read them and the Osho Zen cards do. I have found it best to just go with it, because if I try to read the deck that does not want to be read, the cards become blank to me.

"I did once buy a deck called the Dance of Life Tarot. I found them intriguing and love the folk art type of artwork, but still to this day I cannot read those cards. I have no idea why, but every once in a while I will pull them out and try to read them and get nothing. Maybe I am not ready for them at this time…"

As Tiffany has become more connected with her cards, her accuracy has increased, and she has sometimes been astounded. "When the first reading I gave myself actually happened — which involved a move to another state – I was blown away. I had recorded my readings on paper and didn't refer to it for months, forgot about it, even."

She first read for someone other than herself around 2000, when she read for her husband and her mother, neither of whom had much belief in the power of the cards. Her husband has since become her biggest supporter, once he saw how accurate she can be.

In 2002, Tiffany and her husband began hosting a weekly tarot night with two friends. Her readings seemed to be more accurate than the other participants, to the point that it made her friends uncomfortable. She documented her readings, and would check back in with her friends to confirm if and when things happened.

She received more calls confirming her predictions than not, which boosted her confidence. She started doing more and more readings, and her husband suggested she start charging for them. She had problems with this at first, and sometimes still struggles with whether she should take money for them.

Clients started to come to her home for readings, and Tiffany eventually found that with four children, it would be easier to do them over the Internet. She began by doing online readings for friends and quizzing them to test her accuracy. She received a lot of positive responses and launched her website, with her husband's help, in January 2010. She now exercises her powers by giving readings to friends in person and via http://www.tarotempress.biz. She also does whimsical portraits of spirit guides.

Despite her online presence, Tiffany says most of her neighbors and the parents of her children's friends don't know about her special abilities. "I share my experiences in a guarded manner, checking people's responses and gradually revealing more and more."

Readings and Reactions

People visit psychics to get clarity on situations they are having trouble understanding or acting upon. They want to know about love, money, sex, parents, friends, lovers, and even their pets.

Tiffany believes her abilities are best used to help people who are lost or stuck in life to move forward. "I seem to do well with finding the hang-ups people have, but avoid getting to the root cause," she says. "My readings are about empowerment for the individual. I offer counseling with my readings as well, since it is important to me that the client understand their messages and what areas they need to work on in order to move forward. I often encourage my clients to do affirmations and vision boards to find out what they really want out of life. So many times we go through life looking for something, but not really sure what we are looking for. An example would be going shopping for an unknown event. How can you know where to look if you have no clue what you need to buy? I find this to be true with how many go through life — not knowing what they want and missing that special someone when they come along because they were unable to recognize Mr. or Mrs. Right."

A vision board is a visualization tool used to attract things you want into your life. Using items cut from magazines, drawings, and writings, the theory is that by studying these items, you will be able to become who you want to become and your dreams will become reality.

From a societal perspective, she feels her abilities are used to help people learn to recognize happiness and be okay with their struggles, knowing they won't last forever. "I work on changing their attitudes as well," she says. "Happy thoughts bring happy things and we should not fuel the fire of negativity."

However, she says she does sometimes tune into the darker side of people, and that can be uncomfortable. A friend confessed many months after such a reading that she had been in a very bad place and did not want Tiffany to know, but that it had helped her look at her life differently and begin to make positive changes.

Tiffany says she has come to learn that reading tarot is not "one size fits all," and that sometimes she has read for people and did not connect with them, and so she was unable to get accurate information from the cards.

Some readings stand out in her mind. "When I was first coming out of the 'psychic closet' to friends, I gave a reading to a neighbor. I told him he would meet a woman and they would have a relationship. About six months later, he called to tell me he had met someone special and they did have a relationship for several years."

Another early reading involved one of her husband's co-workers, who was having relationship problems. "We were able to uncover a lot of good and bad things going on in her life, and one of the bad things was the current relationship, which just was not right for her. The cards told me that she would meet a man in six months who would be unlike anyone she had dated before. She did meet this man six months to the day. We got together for another reading and I told her she would marry this man in the summer. She married him in June. She has been very happy in this relationship, and her life has blossomed in many other ways as well."

Sometimes readings present difficulties — how much information is too much information? How do you know what to say and not say?

This question came into play when one friend came to her for a reading. Tiffany pulled her cards and read in them that she was having marital problems — the love was falling away. "I allowed reason to come into play here, disregarded my intuition and the messages I was getting, and told myself that this could not be true and I couldn't tell this woman such a thing. I have no idea why I allowed this to happen, but I did, and I told her that her husband was very supportive of her going back to school, which he was. But the key to the reading was the card telling of marital problems.

"After I finished my reading, she looked disappointed and told me she was not happy with her husband and was not sure if she wanted to stay married to him. I never let that sort of "reasoning" happen to me during a reading again. That was a huge lesson for me, and so, no matter how strange or crazy a reading may seem to me, I tell what I see, feel, or hear. Period."

And how about negative information in the cards? Tiffany told me that when, in a reading, she finds someone is really struggling or in extremely difficult circumstances, she tries to find a positive way to deliver the information. She doesn't believe in leaving someone with negative news or thoughts, which she feels can add to their confusion and possibly frighten them.

"I find a way to offer a resolution to their circumstance," she says. "It is very important to me that they do see the light at the end of the tunnel with their problems or concerns, even if it means they will continue to struggle for a while longer."

Tiffany says she gets the most joy out of helping someone move forward. When she correctly interprets a message from a spirit and that person gets what was intended for them in order to move forward, that is pure joy to her. She told me, "Just recently I gave a girl in the United Kingdom a reading regarding her cat that had passed over before Christmas 2009. I was able to relay messages to her that had great meaning. She told me she had been smiling all day because of my reading. That was such a blessing — I felt so honored at that moment that I have a small part in making her happy."

Friends and Family

Tiffany says some people respond to her pronouncements as though everything she reveals is invented by someone with an overactive imagination, or they question her belief system. Her goal is to educate them. People can be educated, though, only if they want to be, and revealing your inner spiritual life to others can be risky.

Tiffany described one negative experience. "A friend on Facebook sent me an email message telling me I was playing with the Devil and should stop playing with Tarot cards. I found it interesting that this person never once asked me anything about what I do, but just assumed the bad experience they related as happening to them was sure to be mine as well."

The Facebook friend told her that everything she was doing was wrong, all the while telling her how much she loved her. Tiffany ended the exchange by telling the person that they would have to agree to disagree, and wanted to move on from there. The person made no effort to try to get past their differences, and eventually dropped her from their friend list. The other sides of this coin are people who only want to be Tiffany's friend or to know her better because she is psychic, more than who she is otherwise.

Nothing frightens Tiffany about her abilities, although she is concerned that someone may try to harm her because they believe what she does is related to the Devil, or go off the deep end because they hated their reading or didn't understand it.

Also, she tells me, "I do sometimes feel guilty when I know or sense personal things about others. I'm talking about people who haven't asked me for a reading. An example would be a friend I reconnected with recently. She has become very religious, but was not this way when we knew each other many years before. I sensed she was trying to be part of what her new husband expected her to be with regards to his religion. It just felt that she was going through the motions but desperately was missing what her heart wanted her to be, which be unacceptable to her new husband."

But, the woman had not asked for a reading, so Tiffany did not relay the message. She was validated later, though, when the two women had a brief conversation and her friend related how she had to work hard on her new faith and that sometimes she missed her previous belief system.

Sometimes, friends are lost without any real explanation. Tiffany and a woman became friends around 2004 when they met at a children's birthday party — Tiffany's daughter was in the same class as the woman's son. "This was around spring, just as school was about to end for the year. Later, my daughter had a birthday swim party and we invited the class. She was one of the only moms to come and stay for the party and to actually go for a swim. I thought she was interesting, because most moms would never dream of going swimming at a birthday pool party, but instead are eager to leave for the two hours of freedom!

"We had a chance to talk, and she and her son stayed for a few hours after the party. We became best buddies and talked on the phone, went shopping and visited each other, and even trained for and ran a marathon together. We even decided to make jewelry together, and did a craft show at the church I was attending at the time. Then I became pregnant, and very involved in my readings. I had other friends that read tarot, and my husband had bought a deck of cards and we all four would get together for weekly tarot night.

"At some point, I gave my friend a reading during the tarot night, and after a period of time asked for her to help with the accuracy since I was doing the reading without her present. I only asked it was a hit or a miss. She replied it was a miss, and I asked her to explain. The explanation was that I told her she would be earning a lot of money soon. She became the president for the PTA and ended up doing that for two years in a row because she earned the school a lot of extra money. Because she personally didn't make the money for herself, she called the reading a miss, and she never talked to me again. I called her a few times, but she would not take my calls or return them. I had the baby and called her, and she still never called or even acknowledged the baby and I finally took the hint and tossed her number. It was very disappointing to say the least. I still to this day do not know what happened."

Tiffany says her real friends accept her for who she is, and her abilities aren't the main topic of conversation — they are too busy talking about other things going on in their lives.

Her children know that she reads tarot cards and that she can sense spirits, but that's the beginning and the end of that until they get older. Tiffany says that all of her children have the ability to be intuitive. Her oldest son, she believes, is an empath — he's very sensitive to moods and intonations. Her third child once told her he saw a man in his room with blood all over him; Tiffany believes he will become a medium. "My daughter asks a lot of questions, and just recently had a paranormal experience when visiting Alcatraz." As for her youngest, he seems to always know where things are hidden; when she was pregnant with him, a psychic told her that the boy would be very psychic indeed.

What it means to be psychic

Tiffany believes anyone can learn to be psychic; that it's our birthright as humans, although she doesn't believe we can all attain a high level of psychic ability. She uses as an example differing abilities at mathematics: "Some people come into this world just seeming to know things like math. Numbers always make sense to them, and they always excel at math or anything with numbers. I think the same is true in learning how to use our psychic abilities. Some people will work years trying to develop very basic skills, while others will be born at a level that just seems off the charts. I do believe almost everyone can experience their own level of psychic ability."

For those wishing to further develop their own psychic ability, Tiffany recommends reading anything you can find on psychic development, and find a reputable psychic to teach you what you need to know if you want to do readings. Metaphysical stores often hold classes in tarot reading or development of psychic gifts.

One question I asked everyone is: Do you feel "chosen"?

Tiffany responded: "I do feel 'chosen,' and because I feel chosen to do this job, I have a responsibility to myself, to the Universe, and to anyone who chooses me for a reading to be the best I can be. Trust me, there are times when I am tired of trying to explain for what seems like the millionth time, a section of a reading to someone so they will get their message, but it is my job to make sure that everyone who comes to me understands their reading. I try my very best to follow up on readings that are sent out to make sure they did get their reading and understood their reading. This is all I can do but I know I have given my best to each client and that is what I have been chosen for, I believe."

She adds, "I want people to know that psychics are not God, either. We do not pretend to be God or be closer to God than anyone else.

"I also would like others to know that we psychics are rather ordinary people. We have a recognized gift (similar to playing an instrument or writing a book, etc…) and have studied our gift or found a teacher to help instruct us, much like everyone else learning or trying to improve upon a talent. I want people to know that not all psychics are bad and only out to con people out of their money. I want people to know that psychics have feelings too, and that we raise children and contribute to the community just like everyone else."

You can contact Tiffany at www.tarotempress.biz.

Chapter 3
About the Tarot

I'm going to be deliberately vague here. Tarot is an extremely deep subject. Those who read tarot walk an individual path, and what a card means to one will differ with another. Everyone who reads tarot will individualize card layouts in a way that makes the most sense to them. If you want to learn more about tarot, there's some great information on the web. One great place to see and read reviews on lots of different tarot decks is http://www.aeclectic.net/tarot/*. There also is a section for beginners:* http://www.aeclectic.net/tarot/books/beginners.shtml*. "Tarot for Yourself" by Mary K. Greer is an excellent book for those wanting to use the tarot for personal transformation, rather than reading for others.*

The origins of the tarot are muddled. Depending on which source you choose, it either originated in the thirteenth, fourteenth or fifteenth century, in Europe, Italy, France or Egypt.

One website says that tarot cards are an early form of today's playing cards, entering Europe in the 14th century in Italy and France. One of these supposed early decks, the 15th century Visconti-Sforza Tarocchi Deck, is still available today.

For practical purposes, since there are many different tarot decks, all references to suit and major arcana names are those used by the Rider-Waite, said by several sources to be the most popular deck in use today by people in the English-speaking world.

There are 78 cards, with suits representing the hearts, diamonds, clubs and spades of an every-day poker deck. These suits are cups, pentacles, wands and swords, respectively, for the tarot. There are cards that number one through ten for each suit. Jacks are represented by Knights, Kings as Kings, and Queens as Queens. In addition, there is the card of the Page, which comes after ten and before the Knight.

The additional 22 cards are knows as the Major Arcana. Many of the Major Arcana cards show an archetypal figure. Some of these archetypes might include: a warm nurturing mother, a person of authority, a traditional religious leader, or a magical, mystical, or mysterious figure. Archetypes are represented by renderings of people or as abstract symbols. Known as the "heart of the tarot" to many readers, the Major Arcana cards are thought to represent the strengths, hopes, fears, weaknesses and triumphs of humanity.

There are many, many tarot decks. I own about twenty, mostly because I like the different art (most tarot decks are beautiful), but also because different decks seem to resonate with different issues. Some readers use specific decks to answer specific questions.

Everyone I speak with who reads tarot cards (including myself) has a favorite deck. It might be their first deck, it might not, but it's always the deck that "speaks" to them and the one they find easiest to interpret.

Cards are laid out using various "spreads," where the position of the card is given a specific meaning. One of the most popular spreads is the Celtic Cross, which is made up of 10 or 11 cards, depending upon whether or not one uses a "significator," which is a card chosen to represent the seeker.

The spread above is a Celtic Cross spread, with a significator, using the Rider-Waite deck.

The positions of the cards are read as follows:

1. The first card is the significator if used. Otherwise it represents the general tone of the issue at hand.
2. The second card goes on top of the first to indicate the basic problem, obstacle or antagonist.
3. The third card shows the foundation of the issue: worries, desires, influences etc.

4. The fourth card shows the immediate past, what led the seeker to the current situation.

5. The fifth card "crowns" the situation. It is the goal, the dreams.

6. The sixth card is the immediate future. This is not the final outcome, simply the next step on the journey.

7. The seventh card represents the seeker and how they approach the situation.

8. The eighth card represents the seeker's immediate surroundings - house, workplace, people, etc. and how they effect the situation.

9. The ninth card represents hopes and fears. It can be the best or the worst. It can represent aspiration or warning.

10. The tenth card is the final outcome. It must, of course, be read in conjunction with the other cards in the spread.

As far as interpreting the cards is concerned, most tarot decks come with a booklet explaining the meaning of individual cards, but to do a reading, you must know the meanings of the cards as they related to each other. It's like pieces of a puzzle or a series of photographs, when put together, tell a story.

The one book I can recommend for basic tarot meanings for the Rider-Waite deck is *Mastering the Tarot*, by Eden Gray. Published in 1973, it still gets rave reviews as a guide to self-teaching the tarot.

Chapter 4
Jason Lindo

Jason Lindo, a sensitive, is a Jew who grew up in Hawaii, where, he says, everyone believes in ghosts. And, as with some of the other subjects in this book, it's all in the family.

I met Jason in 2004, when he accompanied a group of ghost hunters to my bookstore. He was able to communicate with the spirit of a German shopkeeper there, as well as the other spirit inhabitants. We subsequently attended some investigations and ghost conferences together. He's also a good friend of Dee Disparti, another subject in this book.

He has been a hospice social worker for the Sacramento AIDS Foundation and is now a supervisor with a large social service agency, where he is a case management supervisor. He is 52 years old.

Jason grew up in Honolulu, hearing tales of supernatural experiences that happened to family members. Some of the stories were several generations old, so there was no stigma attached, and no "coming out" about his ability to see and sense spirits. Whenever he had an experience, he would simply tell his grandparents, who would try to interpret it for him.

His realization of his abilities came early. His sisters says he had imaginary friends, two older women he called Chlora and Chleena, with whom he used to have conversations. Both of his sisters can see spirits, and his oldest sister believes that the women were not imaginary, but the spirits of two women who were watching over him when he was young, most likely because he had very bad asthma, which kept him in and out of hospitals as a child.

When Jason was five years old, his maternal grandparents began taking him to visit the family graves on his mother's side. "I was the youngest in the family, and the Hawaiian tradition is the youngest child is allowed to be raised in part or completely by the grandparents," he explains. "Among the reasons for this is for the elders to pass down the family history and traditions. Visiting the family graves is a very important tradition."

They were visiting at the old Luke Society Chinese cemetery on the slopes of the Punchbowl, an extinct volcano that has a veterans' cemetery in the crater. Jason's great-grandmother, a member of the Hawaiian royal court – a lady-in-waiting to the last queen - and his stepfather, a Chinese immigrant, are buried there. They parked near the gate, where his grandparents went to a spigot to fill the coffee cans with water for flowers.

Jason remembers, "I ran ahead, and when my grandparents caught up to me, they found me standing in front of my great-grandmother's grave. I had never been there before, and my grandmother asked me how I knew where her grave was located. I told her that I had seen a woman dressed in a white muumuu. I thought she was my grandfather's youngest sister, Leilani, who we all called Aunty Babe. When I got close to the woman, I realized she looked a lot like Aunty Babe, but I knew she wasn't.

"She was solid, like a living person, and she was standing behind this tombstone. She smiled at me, and then slowly disappeared. I thought she was hiding. I described her in detail, and my grandmother told me calmly that was my great-grandmother, Cecilia Ku'ualoha Kaha'opulani Ka'upena. I had inherited my asthma from her. My mother's Hawaiian name, Ku'ualoha, was given to her because my great-grandmother had died several months before my mother was born. My grandmother told me that since this was my first time visiting her grave, she was there to say aloha to me and welcome me as a grandchild she had never met. To them, it was perfectly natural that I saw her."

Jason's grandparents simply told him not to be afraid. And he wasn't.

As a child, he also discovered that he had the ability to tell when a storm was coming. He would also see in his mind's eye, and sometimes physically, spirits in the homes of relatives and friends.

"I always told my family members, as it is considered a gift that many people have among Native Hawaiians, to see or sense spirits, so there is no stigma involved in talking about it," says Jason. "I have had relatives ask me to come over to their home to see if I can sense a spirit or to bless the house or to communicate with the spirit. I pick and choose what I disclose to friends because I have had friends either come right out and accuse me of making up what I am sensing, or become upset that I told them I sense a spirit in their home, and have never invited me back. I have had some friends since high school who have asked me to try to communicate with the spirits that haunted their homes."

People on both sides of Jason's family share the same abilities. His paternal great-grandmother was a Portuguese *curandeira*, or folk healer, and almost everyone on his Hawaiian maternal grandfather's side of the family are sensitive in some way. His

Portuguese maternal grandmother and her family were also psychic. The Portuguese members of his family are descendants of Marranos, or crypto-Jews, who hid their faith and pretended to be Catholics in order to not break the law and go before the Inquisition. They maintained a lot of the spiritual and folk beliefs in the Sephardic tradition, which Sephardic Jews who were able to practice their religion openly have stopped believing.

Today, Jason uses his abilities to aid ghost-hunting groups and perform house blessings.

Adventures with the Other Side

Jason primarily feels spirits. "They are energy, and create a strong pressure in the middle and small of my back," he says. "I also visualize them in my mind, and sometimes I can hear them. I rarely see apparitions. There are smells that I get, and often I will feel pain or nausea similar to the symptoms of what the person died from; so, shortness of breath and chest pain for someone who had a lung or cardiac condition, for example."

He has learned to close down his abilities when necessary, and always when he is at work. When he was younger, and particularly in junior high, contact with the spirit world was fast and furious. "I remember being told, 'Just tell them to go away. Tell them to go! Don't acknowledge them.'" Two others gave him the same advice. "One was my cousin, who has since passed away and was a *kahuna*. My late cousin was many things, but one of them was a *kahuna pule* and a *kahuna ho'ailona* — a person who can be called upon to offer prayers that become conduits of energy and can affect a person (*kahuna pule*). He was called upon to offer prayers to make people well, get rid of bad dreams, bless houses and dispel spirits. He was also able to interpret dreams and signs in nature; *ho'ailona* is a sign or premonition. I would go to him and say that a spirit that I encountered somewhere frightened me. He would always say, "Don't you know how to be firm with them?

Tell them to leave you alone, swear at them if you have to, but don't be scared of them if they are truly ghosts."

Jason told me that Hawaiians believe in many types of spiritual beings, and his cousin was referring to wondering, restless spirits called either *lapu* or *wailua*. The other advisor was his *hanai* (adopted) aunty. I was visiting my *hanai* auntie, who happens to live here in Sacramento, but was born on Maui, and she says the same thing, "Keli'i, (part of my Hawaiian name that people use as a nickname for me as my Hawaiian name is long, Keli'inohokula,) throw them down in front of you or behind you, but no let them bother you." When they talk about throwing a spirit in front of you or behind you it means to send them back to wherever they came from — to expel them.

Occasionally, though, shutting things off is difficult. "When I worked as a hospice social worker, it was hard, because I could sense death around some clients and knew that their passing was imminent," he says. "I also volunteer for the Chevra Kadishah, the Jewish burial society, in my area. We wash and casket the body 24 hours after death and, if asked, sit with the body in the coffin until the services the next day. I have had a couple of spirits follow me back after doing their taharah (washing). I always do a Hawaiian purification ritual of sprinkling myself with water mixed with sea salt, and the Jewish ritual of washing my hands (we all do this who participate in a taharah) before we leave the funeral home. Both rituals are designed to break that psychic tie that may have happened during the washing of the body."

When he was a hospice social worker for the Sacramento AIDs Foundation, Jason saw a lot of death. Some incidents stand out. There was the time when he was at home. It wasn't his shift, but someone he had gotten to know was close to death. He heard a disembodied voice say, "You have to come over today." Jason drove across town. "As soon as I walked in the door, a staff member told me that they were going to start calling people. The patient died 10 minutes later."

He has seen several clients after they died, including his best friend, Tim. "I was living in San Francisco," he recalls. "I was thinking about him at dinner. I got up and went into the restroom and looked in the mirror. There was Tim's face. The next day I called, and, yes, he had died. The same sort of thing happened when my grandfather died as well."

In another experience, he had a client, Mike, who he would help bathe. Mike would support himself by leaning on Jason. "I was in the shower, and I felt a hand on my shoulder. I said, 'Mike, this isn't the way to say goodbye, but if you're in trouble, hang on as long as you want.' The sensation ended almost immediately." In that way, Jason knew his friend had no trouble crossing over.

Jason says his encounters with spirits during paranormal investigations are completely different. Most of these are what investigators call residual hauntings – trace or place memories. These spirits are more residual energy than an intelligent presence. Other common encounters include those who have an attachment to the place they are haunting, or are not fully aware they are dead.

Other investigations are more active. Among the incidents that stand out: "When I did the *Dead Famous Live* television program, with Dee and Russ Disparti," he says. "We did a séance at the Hollywood Forever Cemetery by Valentino's grave, and we had an apported object appear during the séance." (More on that can be found in the chapter on Dee Disparti.)

"Another was an investigation up near Auburn, CA, with American Paranormal Investigation, when we encountered a demonic force that was disturbing several tenants in an apartment building. We saw red eyes in a cedar tree, heard brush breaking, and got nauseated at one point during the investigation. We caught some good EVPs (electronic voice phenomena) — great investigation.

"In Virginia City, Nevada during a walk around town, I experienced chest pains in the middle of the street, staggered to the sidewalk, and had to sit down. I learned a homeless Vietnam vet with schizophrenia had been shot there a few weeks earlier at the same spot in the street; he died on the sidewalk where I had to sit down."

Jason began ghost hunting 14 years ago, when he met several people who investigated the paranormal. He joined a local group that later broke up, and today works with American Paranormal Investigators.

Paranormal television is filled with "provoking" — insulting or taunting spirits to make them "perform" for the camera. Non-televised investigation groups do it as well, but it's not part of Jason's technique. "I really have trouble with that, because it was someone's mother or grandmother or father or uncle. Would you speak to anyone like that in life? Then why do it to the dead?"

There's also much talk of "demons" in some groups. Jason says he had he never heard of a demonic entity until he came from Hawaii to California to go to college. "During a few investigations, I encountered negative forces. I don't attribute that to evil intent. Can they do evil? Of course. Does that make them evil? Of course not."

Some "demonic" experiences, he says, often have to do with a lack of defenses. "It's very important to protect yourself. You have to have spiritual discipline. If you are not disciplined, you can get hurt mentally — get depressed, irritable, no energy, etc." People can get physically hurt. During one investigation, three people saw a fellow team member picked up and slammed into a wall by some sort of energy. Another man became extremely ill, and the car he was riding in was extraordinarily cold inside the whole way home.

Protection rituals are personal, Jason says, and people should create their own. "It's very important to protect yourself from negative energy," he emphasizes. "If you do not ground and protect yourself and you do this kind of (psychic) work, you are a fool. It is like a doctor going into surgery without scrubbing up first – you will hurt both yourself and the people you are there to help. It also is part of the discipline of paranormal investigations as a sensitive and I do not believe it is optional if you want to do this type of work."

Bless This Home

Another way Jason uses his abilities is through a general house blessing ritual Hawaiians call *pikai.*

"We take a wooden bowl, fill it with fresh water, add unrefined sea salt and fresh turmeric juice (this is optional). We use a Ti leaf, which is a plant we use for traditional medicine and to bring about spiritual balance and protection. I then pray over the water, asking God, the angels, and my ancestors to be present and to work with the water to cleanse and bring peace to each room in the house.

He continues, "I then go through the house clockwise, and sprinkle water with the Ti leaf in each room, starting and ending at the front door. I sprinkle the people living in the house. I do a closing prayer, then I look into the water.

"If there was an evil presence, the water will have bits of almost mucus-like substance in it, or the water will be cloudy. If it is clear, that is a good sign that nothing truly evil was in the home. I then take the water out the front door, command all that is evil and in the water not to return, and throw the water into the street and return to the house without looking back."

Some further rituals are added if it is a cleansing due to an evil spirit. Jason doesn't discuss those cultural practices in a public forum because, if they are done wrong, it could make the situation worse. You also have to be given permission to do them: "My great-aunty and another elder, who was a Hawaiian kahuna and minister, are the ones who gave me permission to do pikai when I was 16 years old, back in Honolulu." Nor will he talk about specific house cleansings, because, for Hawaiians, these are private matters, and are not discussed without the permission of the family who asked for them to be done.

Protection comes into play for a house blessing, just as with a paranormal investigation. Jason uses visualization, and carries a Ti leaf with salt in it. He also asks for protection from God and asks his ancestors to be with him.

As for the spirits he finds, he leaves them be, and doesn't encourage them to "go into the light," as the common phraseology has it. "No, unless I am asked, I do not urge them to go into the light. Both Judaism and Native Hawaiian belief say that some spirits are either allowed to remain for a particular reason or lesson, or have been given the opportunity to choose to come back. Others are waiting for their appointed guide to cross them over. Unless I am asked to when I bless the house, or the spirit asks to be helped, I do not believe it is my place to do that. It would be presumptuous of me - in Hawaiian, we say it would be *maha'oe*." *Maha'oe* is a one of those things that a Hawaiian never wants to be called, Jason explains. *Maha'oe* has several meanings, but the gist of it is pushy, rude, nosey, stuck up. or trying to be a know-it-all.

Friends and Family

Because he's Hawaiian, Jason says, he hasn't been made to feel different because of his abilities. "It's no different than being left-handed." After all, he believes his abilities are hereditary from both sides of his family, and were nurtured by the culture he grew up in.

Jason's abilities make his husband, Michael, nervous. He grew up in a family that never talked about the paranormal. "He's very encouraging of my paranormal investigating, but he doesn't like to talk about it," Jason says. "On occasion, he will ask me, usually when something unusual happens in our home, if someone is 'visiting.'"

Growing up, no one ridiculed Jason's abilities, "In Hawaii, as I said, it was no big deal and none of my school friends growing up ever reacted negatively, I only experienced that kind of reaction here in California." They would scoff, and say they didn't believe in ghosts, but he noticed that these were the same people who wouldn't go near the neighborhood's reputedly haunted house.

Inspiration and Putting Abilities to Good Use

I asked Jason if there was anyone who inspires him to use his abilities. He mentions several relatives, particularly his late maternal grandmother and his oldest sister, who is still "very practical" about it. "A couple of good friends, Dee Disparti, an excellent psychic and sensitive I know who now lives in Carolina; Loyd Auerbach, a well-known parapsychologist I have had the privilege of working with; my late cousin, Carl Naluai Jr., who was both a traditional Hawaiian spiritual healer as well as the chazzan (cantor) at my synagogue and a student of Kabbalah; some very close personal friends in the Pagan community; and a couple of authors I have met who have really inspired me for various reasons: Jeff Belanger, Michelle Belanger, Hans Holzer, Elliot O'Donnell, Peter Underwood, Dennis Hauck, Janice Oberding (a wonderfully talented author and investigator and a very supportive, humble individual), Antonio Garcez.

"And then there is the author who, way back in fourth grade, first inspired me to think about collecting ghost lore and seeing this not just as something that happens to me, but a part of a discipline: Sybil Leek, the famous British witch and psychic. I had the honor of meeting her when I was a young teenager."

Jason thinks his abilities are best used to help others: to help those in fearful situations feel comfortable again in their homes and personal lives; to help people come to terms and find peace with the spiritual reality that there is life after death, and that that world does interact with our own; to help spirits who ask for help; and to restore balance to a particular place.

Finally, he says, “I think it is important to help others with the same abilities to know that they are just that: abilities. They are nothing to be afraid of, provided you are respectful of them and do not do rash or risky things with those abilities, like calling up spirits or unnecessarily provoking them, and that the person experiencing them is not crazy.”

Being able to help people, to put their minds at ease and take away any fear they have is among his greatest joys, he says. The experience of being assured that there is something beyond this life brings him great joy.

As for those who want to follow the path of the sensitive? “Read, read, read,” he urges. “Find a sensitive you trust and talk to them. Even go as far as to ask them to teach you. Learn how to meditate, and create a methodology to ground and protect yourself. Always be respectful of the spirits, the place you are investigating, and the people who live there or use that space. And don’t be a thrill junkie!”

I asked Jason, as I asked everyone in this book, what he wants others to know about people like him. He laughed, and replied, “I am a pretty regular guy who just happens to have the ability to communicate with spirits, and who has been taught to help people who are troubled by them.”

Chapter 5
Dee Disparti

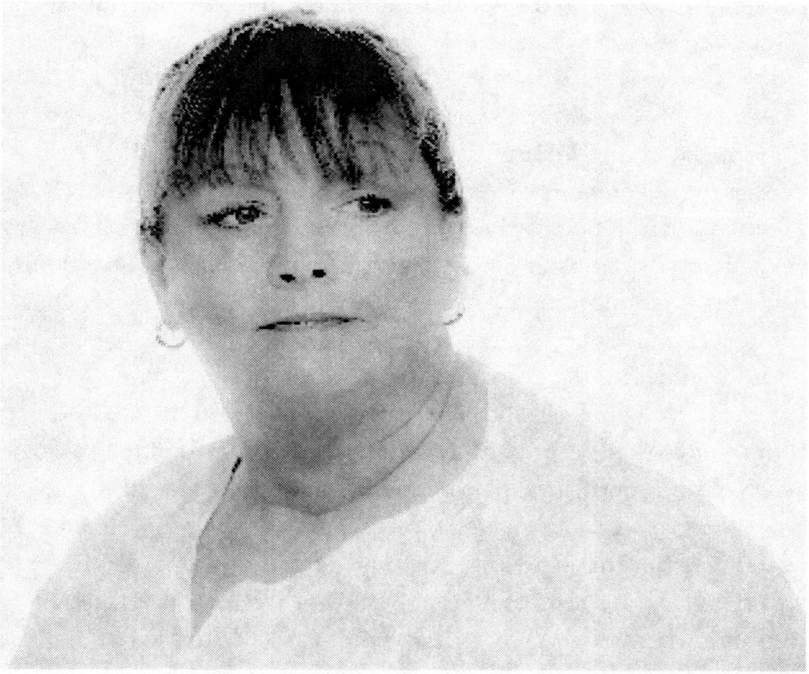

Dee Disparti came into my life when another paranormal investigator brought Dee and her husband, Russ, to investigate my haunted bookstore. Dee is an imposing presence — psychically, physically, and otherwise. She radiates a certain power and a calm self-assurance that can sometimes be intimidating. To know Dee is to know that her powers are genuine, they make her humble, and she's happy to share what she knows.

She has been a paralegal, and owned a tearoom and construction company with Russ. She currently teaches classes, writes, and heals people using the help of spirit doctors and Reiki. She also does private readings.

Like some others in this book, Dee's abilities run in the family. "My Grandmother Wainscott was very psychic," she says. "She would start cleaning house and cooking because a relative was on their way to visit. No one would call or send a letter to let her know they were coming. They all knew she would be ready for them when they arrived. I can never remember her being wrong."

When Dee was age three or four, her grandmother taught her how to use a pendulum, in the form of a needle and thread, to determine the gender of an unborn child.

After that, Dee says, her grandmother treated her as if she was special and began listening to what was happening with the young girl, and explaining the psychic side of life.

From the time Dee was very young, a tall man in a robe made entirely of white light stood at the foot of her bed each night. A hood covered his face, and two other beings stood on each side of him. "I always just thought of them (these other beings) as dogs, as I had no other frame of reference," she says. "I still don't know what they were, but they were also made of white light." The tall figure told her that he was there to protect and watch over her. He was there nightly until she was 12 or 13; there was no question in her mind that he would keep her safe.

Dee doesn't know what it's like not to be psychic — it's normal to her, and she takes it in her stride. She isn't sure how to explain the things that happen to her. She's a friend of Jason Lindo, another subject in this book, and they often share experiences. "A handful of years ago, I was talking to Jason about something I had seen and he called it a vision," she says. "Well, until that time, I had never thought of it that way. I can sit in my office and 'see' what is going on at a great distance while talking to someone, and I didn't realize until just a few years ago that this is called remote viewing."

Dee has studied, taken classes, asked for guidance, and walked the psychic path, which has not been without roadblocks. "The first time I spontaneously went into a trance state, I called the minister of a spiritualist church we attended. He told me that I couldn't be doing what I was doing because I hadn't had the proper training. I found that very strange. If the Universe wants us to do something, we will do it, even without so-called proper training."

For Dee, the whole world is her paranormal oyster. She describes being a psychic medium as being like a lighthouse — a veritable homing beacon. "Even when you shut yourself down, spirits come to see what is going on. Some come wanting help. Most come just to see what is happening."

She does readings by phone and in person. She considers things like tarot cards, and pendulums, etc., as tools to help her focus on the information she is receiving. Tea leaves are her favorite — "I love to read tea leaves because there are so many surprises in every cup," she says. She seldom remembers the readings she gives, because the messages are not for her: "They are just too much to add to what I'm already carrying around."

Jason Lindo mentioned to me that Dee was "excellent with psychometry," so I asked her about it. Psychometry is a form of extrasensory perception characterized by the ability to make relevant associations from, or "read," an object of unknown history by making physical contact with it. It's thought that objects have an energy field that transfers knowledge regarding their history. Sometimes they retain the energy of the person who owned them.

"I like to 'feel' the environment I am in with my hands," Dee says. "I get a lot of impressions and pictures telling a story. I think that is why I like this activity so much — it gives the history of a person or place. This helps me to truly understand that is happening at the time I am there, and gives me clues about how I can help with the situation at that particular location. When I quiet myself, pictures and information come to me when I touch something."

Dee has been inspired throughout her life by her grandmother, the witch Sybil Leek, and the author Marianne Williamson, as well as her husband, Russ, who goes with her on many of her adventures into the paranormal. "It is so good to have someone who understands what is happening and what he needs to do in order to see events come to a positive resolution." She thinks her abilities may have helped to strengthen her marriage: "He's a great sounding board and the strongest supporter in my life." Her two daughters (she also has two stepchildren) have abilities, but only the youngest has any interest, and not much at that. "It's a little sad, because I hate to die and let all I know not continue forward in new generations."

Ghost Hunting

When Dee was very young, she started helping spirits cross over to the other side. No one called it ghost hunting back then, she says: "That's a new label someone put on it. There have always been people doing the same thing I do without all the fanfare attached to it." About fifteen or twenty years ago, she wanted to see if she could intentionally take pictures of spirits and other anomalies. Spirits, in the form of orbs or even apparitions, will sometimes show up randomly in photographs.

"Amazingly," she says, "the first time I asked the spirits for a photograph, I got one. It gave new dimensions to what I was able to do, and made it even more interesting for me."

Dee is a rarity among mediums in that she has materialized an apport — and on television, no less! An apport is the paranormal transference of an article from one place to another, or an appearance of an article from an unknown source, and is often associated with poltergeist activity or séances.

The television series was *Dead Famous*, the location Hollywood Forever Cemetery. I'll let Dee tell this astounding story in her own words:

"I have to admit one of my favorite places to go is a mausoleum. There is so much activity there, even in the daylight hours, going unnoticed. After dark, when visitors have left, the games begin. If you want to talk to someone of the dearly departed persuasion, this is the time to go and the place to be.

"There is something almost seductive about the feeling of all that cool marble around. The moonlight glistens off the white marble walls and the feeling of being in another time, in another civilization, can overwhelm you if you allow it. Suddenly you could be in ancient Greece, walking through a temple all alone …

"The sound of someone walking in the next corridor brings you back to reality — no sense being in a marble crypt, complete with a production crew who are paying for the facilities, and not taking full advantage of the moment. Off we go — there is work to be done!

"As if by magic, a table and four chairs appear, along with a candle and a lighter. Someone is busy putting camcorders on tripods, and there is hustle and bustle all around. The director is checking the battery of the hand-held camcorder. The séance is about to begin.

"We take our seats and light the candle. The participants in the séance join hands, get comfortable, and off go the lights. An all-important prayer for protection is uttered, and we are off and running. The director then takes her place between us all, with a camcorder held in her hands to get those all-important close-ups.

"We have been told we are looking for Rudolph Valentino, and he does not appear to be interested. For a good fifteen or twenty minutes we ask for Mr. Valentino to visit us but nothing — nary a word nor sign.

"We change tactics and ask for a sign of anyone in the area who is with us from the other side. [Network actor] Peter Finch appeared before me, laughing like a man who had just been the originator of an excellent joke. He was certainly a cocky spirit and seemed full of himself.

"Suddenly comes the sound of hushed male voices chattering as if they are in a men's club — this went on for twenty or thirty seconds. I'll mention here that there were crypts all the way to the ceiling, and the window was a huge stained glass one that neither opened nor closed. Behind us was the small production crew, and there was no way for the sound to have come at us from the direction it did unless it was from out of nowhere. At this point, it was really getting to be fun. And when you have a lucky streak going, you try to multiply your luck. And so we did.

"Our director keeps asking to get more. Never timid when it comes to a challenge, we, in the circle, asked for more. We were once again treated to an otherworldly noise. A long, low, masculine, very loud moan began to usher forth from nowhere. How cool is that?

"By this time Peter Finch was slapping his knees and laughing so hard he could barely stand. It was fun indeed for all of us. With a little push from the director, once again, we pushed forward for some 'real proof.'

"This next portion is hard to believe unless you have been someplace and had it happen to you. So here it goes…

"I am asking for more proof. The director is in my face and then moves to the other side of the table. Our hands are still all upon the top of the table, joined. Our feet can be seen, and Mr. Finch is beginning to develop a gleam in his eyes. I should have known we were headed for rocky waters!

"As soon as the director was standing opposite me at the table, something came out of thin air just above us and ever so gently touched me on the shoulder, then fell to the ground. It was so gentle there was no way it could have been thrown, like someone tapping you on the shoulder. Mayhem ensued and we had to break the circle to calm the director. She was screaming and hopping around. Good old Mr. Finch was about doubled over with laughter. We calmed down the director, sat back down, and our production crew decided it was time to pack up and leave. I guess we had supplied enough 'proof' for one evening.

"To this day, I still have the wonderful quarter moon with a star in my possession. That is what came down from the air that night, the apport that was given to me by a Hollywood movie star. It is blue with sequins, and the star is light in color dangling down from the moon. It will be with me forever to remind me of what can happen when you ask for it."

Since then, Dee says, several things have showed up, and her husband even had an apport while taking a shower — three quarters just fell on him from nowhere!

Another memorable ghost-hunting experience for Dee was an investigation at the Joseph D. Grant house in Grant Ranch Park in Santa Clara County, Calif. A historian accompanying the crew as a docent asked Dee to tell her something about a soldier in a painting. "I heard a very British voice say, 'I am a faggot, you silly cow,'" Dee recalls. "Well, I told the historian that she didn't really want to hear what I had been told." The docent, however, was eager to hear, so Dee told her that the man in the painting was gay.

The stunned woman says she was indeed correct, but that wasn't part of the tour and very few people knew it.

While working to resolve a haunting in the California gold country, Dee was shown a vision of a shaman performing a ceremony. He was chanting and shaking a rattle, and smoke was heavy in the air. There was a heavy, hairy thing opposite the shaman. "I couldn't figure out if it was a bear or a Bigfoot." She described the vision to an anthropologist, who was quite excited — it seems that there is a little-known Cherokee ceremony involving Bigfoot.

"It's so rewarding when you get confirmation you are correct regarding a person or place," Dee says. "It keeps you on track and moving forward."

Haunted Homes

Some of us have lived in haunted houses. Many would not want to do it again. But for Dee, it seems to come with the psychic territory — only one house she has lived in was not haunted. "When we move in, we already have a family waiting for us," she says. "We just set certain ground rules and let them know there is room for all of us. I do insist that our bedroom and bathroom remain off-limits."

Dee and Russ's last house reportedly had "haints," as she describes them, from the time it was built. They heard people milling around the attic during certain times of the month, and saw colored lights there as well. "Interviewing people who had grown up in the area and had spent the night in the house, we found that many of the stories of the hauntings were the same types of experiences we were having," she says.

"After we left the house, we received the weirdest phone call from our real estate agent. It seems he was showing the house and a client wanted to take a look at the attic. The agent waited downstairs and was greeted by a screaming client leaving the house post-haste. It seems a glowing green mask had come after the client as he was taking a look at the attic. Apparently the spirits didn't want him to buy the house! We also discovered handwritten information in pencil on the beams in the attic. It included a warning that the house was haunted. This was left by the first children who lived in the house."

Dee and Russ have ghosts in their current home in North Carolina. "We have an elderly gentleman who smells like he has not had a bath in a while. He likes to linger in the hall, and moves back and forth trying to be where the action is. There is a little old lady who likes to cook and bang pots and pans around in the wee hours of the morning. She waits until the house is quiet before she begins her kitchen chores and is not visible when you go to check on what is happening. You can certainly feel her, though; you could cut the air with a knife, the air is so heavy when she is out and about. We also have a ghost dog that likes to climb up the stairs with its nails clicking, and then it scratches on the upstairs door wanting into the top floor. When you open the door, nothing is there."

Dee continues, "When we first moved into this house, I slept several nights in a chair because of my allergies. I can breathe better in a recliner sometimes. One night, a man came forward threatening me and screaming he was going to send me to hell. He somehow created all kinds of hellfire and brimstone, along with pictures for me so he could scare me. I explained this was all very interesting; however, it was not scary. He moved back and quit being active. He is still around from time to time."

On another occasion, Dee and her family were checking out a historic house in a small town near their own. There were rumors the house was haunted, and curiosity got the better of the owner. As they sat at the dining room table, a young woman dressed in the style of the late 19th century was going back and forth from that room and the kitchen. "She had such a saucy attitude and I was telling the owner about her. At the same time, my daughter was taking pictures and took three of the door to the kitchen. On the second picture she captured a female mooning me. It has provided us with a few laughs!"

When dealing with the paranormal, protection is important. Like many mediums, Dee uses white light. This is a visualization technique whereby you close your eyes and see yourself surrounded by white light that chases away darkness and negativity.

Being psychic, Dee is more vulnerable than most, so she also shuts herself down and then opens herself to outside energies in increments. Even so, spirits do sometimes come home with her, and she must explain that they are not allowed in certain places or rooms. She says they soon get bored and leave in a day or two.

Dee treats these visitors with the nonchalance born of experience. For others, it can be quite traumatic.

"Once we were visiting a graveyard in San Antonio, where a young man was filming a documentary about us on ghost hunting. Before we went to investigate, I was kidding around about looking in the rearview mirror and seeing eyes looking back at you even though you are all alone," Dee says with a chuckle. "When the young man left to go home, a great electrical storm blew into the area. He wouldn't answer his phone for a couple of days, and when he did, he explained he would not be finishing his film or going investigating again, period. As he was driving home, he looked up and saw eyes looking at him from the backseat in his rearview mirror. We'll never know if his imagination ran wild or he had a guest!"

Spirituality

Dee grew up in north Texas; her father was an electrician and her mother a designer and dance instructor. Both of them largely ignored her psychic abilities. They were Christians and also members of the Society of Friends (Quakers). She has chosen to embrace the Universe and God as opposed to any particular religion. "I believe in God and see the Universe as sacred," she says. "I do not believe in religion — to me it seems more a business than anything else." Dee doesn't see her abilities as coming from a divine source, but believes that being psychic is taking what you have been given naturally and by inheritance and working with it. "But who really knows?" she says. For those who are just discovering they have psychic abilities, she advises, "Meditate, meditate, meditate. And pay attention to your hunches. This is the best thing you can do for yourself to tune into what you may be receiving."

Dee is a believer in reincarnation and feels it is a basic tenet of most religions and cultures, and that it was part of the Christian belief system until church elders decided it no longer had a place. She surmises that if you have only one life to live, you will be more likely to tithe and follow the teachings of the church for your salvation. If you have more than one chance, though, why live a life as limited as your church demands?

"I remember the last life before this one," she says. "Primarily the death is what I remember. I was running in London and all was dark. Bombs began to fall and I was crushed to death by a structure falling on me. My mother told me when I was very young, if I heard a large plane overhead, I would find a ditch. Seems I threw myself into the ditch and would put my hands on the back of my neck to protect myself."

Dee adds that when she was a baby and just learning to talk, a neighbor noticed she was speaking Hebrew, rather than English, as though Hebrew was her first language. No one in her family or their circle of friends spoke Hebrew.

As with the other psychics I interviewed, spirit guides play a part in Dee's life. "We all have spirit guides to help us navigate this physical world," she says. "As our needs change, our guides change. We always have guides who can help us in our current situations. In some cases, the spirit guide has lived life or lives in the physical world and some have never occupied a physical body.

They are not there to change anything so much as help us steer in the proper direction. They also often help us through perilous times."

There are times when a guide influences you more than you could possibly imagine. Dee says. About fifteen years ago, a female guide from India come came through to her. She Dee was unaware of her presence until she saw a certain pin in a store. Dee had to have that pin, and had no idea why. It was a Victorian-era gold sari pin. She bought the pin, and then became aware of the guide. "She was always happy I purchased the pin for her," she says. "I still have the pin, and it brings a smile to my face every time I see it."

On Being Psychic

For Dee, being psychic is normal, and what would dismay many people frightens her not at all. She feels she can best use her powers to help others understand theirs and prodding them to use them. She also hopes to give people the tools they need to resolve any problem they might have in their lives, and enjoys healing and helping spirits cross over.

In her classes, she teaches on topics including spiritual subject matter, dowsing, and learning how to investigate the paranormal. All sorts of people attend. They are generally there, she says, to answer questions they have. "The classes are very rewarding, as they allow people to look at their lives and the big picture in a different way," she says. "It opens doors in their minds, allowing them to search, to think about what they have uncovered, and how it can be integrated into their worldview."

Dee sees herself as someone just like everyone else, with a slightly different approach to life. "It's the frauds who give us bad names and make people feel we are strange or scary," she says. "There's nothing magical, mysterious, or scary about us. We are everyday folks and most of us have our feet on the ground. I really dislike the 'Madame Whatevers' who tell the world they are psychic and use the public's needs to take advantage."

What she does, she says, is just what she does, "just like a mechanic fixes things mechanical and a painter paints. I just do something a little different."

You can contact Dee at deedisparti@gmail.com

Chapter 6
Mediums, Psychics, and Sensitives (Oh, my!)

Some psychics are mediums. But not all mediums are psychics. But all mediums and psychics are sensitives.

Psychics are people who perceive information via a "sixth sense," that is, a sense hidden from the normal five senses. This information is gained via what is commonly called extrasensory perception, or ESP. Psychics convey information through various means – tarot or other types of cards, palmistry, crystal balls, and mirror scrying, or by simply concentrating, meditating or praying. They can see or predict events to come.

A **medium** has a direct line to the afterlife. Mediums open themselves to discarnate energy. Some mediums communicate with spirits while fully conscious.

Others are trance mediums — someone who goes into a trance state to relay messages from the other side. This is typically the type of mediumship shown in films and on television.

Sensitives also communicate with the dead and work with active and residual energy . Those who see, hear, touch, taste, or smell spirits are sensitive. The level of perception of sensitives varies, and some are able to communicate in "real time," much as a medium does, conveying messages from the dead. Sensitives include those who are empathic (able to perceive and communicate the emotions of the dead or just an overall atmospheric feeling). Most ghost hunters are sensitive to some degree.

Some famous contemporary psychics include: John Edward, Lisa Williams, James Van Praagh, Sylvia Browne and Mary Ann Winkowski.

Recommended reading: *Small Mediums at Large: The True Tale of a Family of Psychics*, by Terry Iacuzzo, J.P. Putnam's Sons, 2004; *When Ghosts Speak* by Mary Ann Winkowski, Grand Central Publishing, 2007; *Lily Dale: The Town that Talks to the Dead* by Christine Wicker; *Life Among the Dead*, by Lisa Williams, Simon Spotlight Entertainment, 2008.

Chapter 7
Deborah Carr Senger

I met Deborah Carr Senger through my friend and fellow author, Janice Oberding. Deborah describes herself as a historic and spiritual medium. She is a writer and researcher, and owns and operates a tour company with business partner Chris Holtz. They conduct a historic haunted-walking tour in Bloomington, Illinois;, gangster tours, and performances as Lincoln and the Lady, where she dresses as Mary Todd Lincoln. She also hosts live paranormal investigations.

She is the author of Mysteries and Haunts of Central Illinois Part I: McLean County, The Land of Lincoln, Route 66 and Beyond.

Deborah Carr Senger follows her intuition. "I can be a healer, a reader, a psychic detective, a teacher, a student," she says. "I am drawn to wherever I need to be, and allow the messages and energy to use me as their tools."

As a historical researcher and writer, she channels to the source and is led to the stories. As a historical actor, she provides the format to open others to connect with the past. As a paranormal investigator, she says it is not so much the spirit in the house, she said, but the spirit of the energy of the investigation. "As long as I listen to my inner voice, all my abilities are on point in all the settings of my life."

As far back as she can remember, Deborah knew or understood situations and loved being around people. She felt very drawn to some people, and stayed away from others. She describes herself as a "Zen Christian," and says she has always felt loved and filled with the light of God. "I believe I am the vessel and the energy of God's love, and the blessings flow through me to others." Her abilities, she says, come from God the creator and Mother Earth to ground her.

Her mother had her own abilities, and noticed how the young girl was drawn by, and fascinated with, people. She allowed her the freedom to seek and explore. "As young as two or three, I was pulling a wagon and telling my parents I was collecting souls."

Deborah remembers the childhood tea party set swirling around her bedroom as she shared tea with her make-believe friends. She said she knew their names, and as she grew up, and learned about family and friends who had passed, she realized that it was not make-believe — her tea party friends were actually relatives and friends who had passed on.

Her parents knew she had a very active imagination, but actually didn't define her as a medium until she was willing to surrender, herself, to that definition.

"I am now of the mind that there is no such thing as make-believe or imagination, but God communicating and providing us with what we need, including communication with the dead," she says.

As a growing child in Florida, she experienced continued visits from her make-believe friends, observed a fleet of UFOs (one of her brothers confirms this event), and remembers first communicating with alternate life forms. "As a small child, this was just a regular part of my childhood. I did not know it was anything different or unusual," Deborah says.

When Deborah's her family moved to Japan, when she was in eighth grade, she became more aware that her observations were out of the ordinary. "Intrigued, I studied and discovered the mystical worlds further and also checked out my first Sylvia Browne book. I remarked to my mother that I was a lot like her and she agreed."

One early spirit visitation was Andy, a friend of her brother, Mike's, while they were living in Japan. Andy lived in upstate New York. He and had terminal cancer. "When I was a kid," Deborah, says, "spirits usually came to me at the beginning or end of a dream state. Andy came to me with a message for Mike – he was okay, and wanted Mike to know that."

Deborah's family then moved to Hawaii for her last three years of high school. That time, she recalls, was a combination of combined typical teenage pranks with a Ouija board, experiences with magic and spells, and the growing realization that she was aware of events before they happened. She began noticing and giving voice to her abilities and observations about other people's energy. "This was still a very private world of investigation, wonder, and appreciation of all things around me including nature and people."

Learning to Use Her Abilities

Even though she knew she had these abilities, Deborah didn't take her skills seriously until she went through a possibly life-threatening health situation, she didn't take them seriously.

"About sixteen years ago I was diagnosed with a large ovarian cyst," she says. "The doctors believed it was quite serious, and an oncologist was brought in for the surgery. Once I was home recovering, the doctor called to let me know that within a few days the tests would confirm a possibly grim diagnosis. I had a sudden 'ah-ha!' moment about my life and what I had not achieved. With the idea of a limited time on earth, I really began to evaluate my own life's purpose," Deborah tells me.

Fortunately, the news was good. . But the feelings that "aha" moment created remained, and Deborah decided to quit her job in the travel industry and develop her mediumship. She tells me that as soon as she made this commitment, she began to meet those who could help her along her journey.

"Once I made this commitment to my own development as a medium, many wonderful mentors were put in my path. All of these people are still in my life and I continue to bless others and be blessed by their presence in my life. Every April, I reach out to each of these mentors and thank them for finding me."

Once she found her path, traveling it was not always easy.

"I had always used my abilities with others as a fun reading around the kitchen table or fire," she says. "So once I decided to 'come out of the closet,' several close friendships were challenged. Some churches condemn soothsayers and fortunetellers. Many believe that if it is not of God it is indeed of evil. Several friendships were closed down and one particular friend projected, 'I know I am going to lose you to this.'"

But at the same time, the friend would tell people about Deborah's work as a medium, which served to bring her clients, rather than have the intended effect of putting them off. She tried very hard to keep the friendship under the friend's s rules and eventually it fell apart. "I truly believe in the Holy Spirit, and yet am considered 'evil' by opening the energy in healing and energy circles. Once again it is not for me to judge. Perhaps fear dictates opinions."

As she meets new people in working situations, such as ghost investigations or private readings, friendship she is careful to maintain professional boundaries. Deborah wants to be someone's friend because of who she is, not because they want her to "read their mind," she says. "As a spiritual medium, I am led to others that are led to me for spiritual enrichment. It is the balance of knowledge and friendship that develops each relationship with a new acquaintance."

The balance of the spiritual medium and Debbie the person can be a challenge, she muses. She once sponsored a psychic cruise workshop and investigation. One of her readings led to a close relationship and she actually spent several days with this woman, providing readings for many of her friends. This woman was just one in a series of helpful people Deborah soon encountered.

Understanding her abilities is a work in progress. She recalls contacting Janice Oberding of HauntedNevada.com to ask about a private ghost tour of Virginia City. She mentioned in an email to her that she was a medium and often saw dead people. "Janice is so insightful with few words until the moment is right," she recalls. "The first time I met her was at the cemetery outside Virginia City. As I hopped out of the van, she asked, 'What do you see?' It was my first truly confirmable exercise with the paranormal. Every spirit I saw was confirmed through one story or another in Virginia City that day."

She soon was receiving weekly training from with a spiritualist, Gail, who had been recommended by Tom and Lisa Butler, two paranormal researchers who also attended the conference, near her then then-home in North Carolina. Working with Gail showed Deborah how to do healing and energy circle work. Later, while on another psychic cruise, she met Leigh Grace, a psychic from New Orleans. Their friendship has grown and blossomed, and through Leigh's guidance Deborah has learned how to improve her private readings. "It's important to record the session and always emphasize a positive, healthy and happy attitude for me and my client. She, along with Janice and another religious mentor, most importantly, remind me to believe in my true self and the messages."

Readings

As a spirit medium, Deborah's goal is to inspire clients to feel positive in their own spiritual life.

"My readings are very private and personal," she says. "As a spiritual medium, I do not advertise, and believe each person is led to the experience." She tells participants to allow at least two hours for a reading at their "best time of day," and asks them to bring a voice recorder and block off at least two hours. She also prefers that they come alone. "People are more apt to be most open and free to speak and experience without an audience. "However sometimes mother/daughter and husband/wife can create an interesting reading."

Prior to the meeting, she suggests that each client write down some questions. "The energy of the reading is its own entity, and then at the end we uncover the questions, objects (psychometry), and such to see if the answers have already been provided. Many times the questions and more have been provided either in direct or abstract answers. Before the session I spend time inviting spirits to come and join us. I build my energy and am often breathless by the time the person arrives. I often 'spirit write' notes from passed loved ones."

A few years ago, she said, she was working at a convention with Leigh in New Orleans. As she drove into the city from Baton Rouge, she scribbled notes from her conversations with the spirits.

That evening, she did a several five- minute readings and was able to check off each message that had been provided on the trip down.

About nine years ago, Leigh led Deborah to her first "official" reading. "After providing me with a complete reading aboard a Mississippi cruise, she asked me to give her a reading. She taught me much about the techniques of providing a reading — being true to yourself and the message is the most important lesson."

To others with psychic abilities, Deborah shares this advice. "To thy own self be true! Psychic abilities, when properly exercised, enhance *all* of your abilities. Surrender yourself to the Light of Love and Creation and all doors will be opened to you. Open your heart and mind and RUN." She laughs. Be careful."

Deborah limits herself to one or two private readings a week. "During my sessions, I prefer not to be rushed. I prefer my home or theirs. I do have a couple of fun rituals such as Tao cards or my own 'past, present, and future' object readings, but all in all this is used to settle our energies and allow the spirits and messages to enter our sacred space," Deborah says.

She discovers information about her clients by simply and briefly passing her hand underneath theirs. All is revealed. Personality type, love and health situations, and even parallel lives just seem to roll right off from the energy of her hand's passing under another's. With this information, she and the client uncover what is meant to be discovered, she says.

Deborah also has a magic mirror hat has been passed on to her by another psychic, as well as a crystal ball, but these items are used more in workshops and advanced readings. She is guided to use the tools, or not, by the spirits. When she was young, she recalls experimenting with white magic. "I have to admit each spell produced results," she says.

I asked Deborah about some incidents that stand out in her mind. She says that she once saw a woman with a brown and broken aura, and the woman died within a short time. "I must admit I do look at auras of other passengers as I board a plane or elevator." In high school, she did some readings and three of the teens had short lifelines. They all were dead within two years.

On a brighter note, by connecting this side and the other, many of her clients have been able to forgive from beyond the grave, find lost jewelry, follow an Alzheimer's patient's wish for his wife, get pregnant, return to college, and solve crimes.

Her favorite memories of giving readings were when her son was young, they would camp with friends, and late at night she shared her thoughts around the campfire. She never used the term "readings," at this point, because she was just sharing information.

"While in the Carolinas, I was at a 'psychic party,' she recalls. "Each individual was provided ample time for a proper reading. A particular young lady in her 30's was incredibly talented, gifted, and loved yet she was not happy and could not get pregnant. Prior to the event I asked for spirits to come." While talking to this particular young lady, the spirit of a young girl of about 16 appeared to her with her hair in pigtails, wearing pajamas, and eating marshmallows.

"As I described the teen, the client recognized her as her best friend, who had died in a car accident. After further questioning continued, it was revealed that my client was to have been in the car and felt guilty all these years, thinking that she may have saved her friend had she been in the car with her." The dead friend assured her she was happy, loved 'loved! LOVED! LOVED!' Heaven, and asked the woman to get on with her life. Soon after this session the woman became pregnant, named her daughter after her dead best friend, and is now living a fulfilling life, Deborah says.

Mary Todd Lincoln and Historical Tours

I have to confess a personal fascination with Mary Todd Lincoln. She was a strong and talented woman who suffered many losses in her life, and was committed to an insane asylum after accusations leveled by her own son. She also was a believer in spiritualism, and after her son Willie's death, she held a number of séances in the White House. It is said they brought her comfort. And, Abraham Lincoln's ghost is still said to still walk the corridors of the White House.

Deborah shares my fascination, and believes she channels Mary Todd Lincoln.

"As a spiritual medium, " she said, "Spirits are led to me as long as I remain open to the possibility," she says. "Why did I move to Bloomington? Why is Lincoln so important and why do and I my business partner look so much like the Lincolns?

"I do believe Mary Todd Lincoln has been seeking me. I do indeed channel her. She was a spiritualist and believed in séances and communication with the dead. As I research and write, she is indeed right beside me. As I put my hair up and adorn myself with her gowns, I do indeed channel her. Many of my closest friends have commented, 'You are Mary Todd,' when I represent her in our presentations, tours, and walks."

"Mary Todd Lincoln and I do have a special relationship and connection," Deborah said. "I know she brought me to central Illinois," she says. "I know when I dress and put on the makeup and hairdo … she comes alive through me … even my face morphs. People have often remarked how I look so different from myself when I am representing Mary Lincoln."

A local family recently visited Bloomington with of a miniature photo of Lincoln. The story goes that their great-grandfather received this from Mary after the death of Lincoln. Mary spent six weeks at the White House after Lincoln's death going through pictures and memories. She personally wrote letters of thank you to many of Lincoln's colleagues and friends. The note sometimes included a miniature of Lincoln, Deborah tells me.

The minute the photo was placed in her hand, she knew Mary had once held it. "I shook and cried," she recalls. "Mary even let us know she was not at that particular setting or Lincoln's hair would not have been that messy."

"Most often Mary is remembered as 'crazy,' and I know my purpose is to present the true Mary, to the best of my ability. She truly was a well educated, well well-bred 'creature of excitement.' She loved Lincoln and believed in him. Her wedding band from him reads, 'Love is Eternal.' I know when playing the Lincolns my connection to my business partner, Chris Hotz, is special and beyond the moment because of the Lincolns' love for each other."

"Chris and I, as historic actors are sometimes worry about our accuracy in portraying as the Lincolns. Mary kindly reminds me that my intent is pure and to bring the Lincolns alive, as we do, makes her very happy!" One of Deborah's goals is to write a book about Mary Todd Lincoln and bring her the justice and respect she deserves.

When she moved to Bloomington, Illinois, Deborah immediately started work on her first historic ghost tour, with an emphasis on Abraham Lincoln. He spent more than 20 years in and out of the area on the Eighth County Court Circuit, and was asked to consider running for the presidency there, where many of his influential friends lived.

As Deborah researched, wrote, and produced other ghost walks, presentations, and tours, including *Route 66 Ghosts and Gangsters*, and recently the *Wild West Show*, she came to believe that the spirits from the area, such as Bloomington's own "Pawnee Bill" Gordon and William Lillie wanted to be heard, with her as the channel. Also, during the *LIVE! Paranormal Investigations*, she holds, she is usually drawn to a participant and uses to channel a spirit. Recently a family came and she chose a woman who had helped with her father in his last days. He came through during the channeling session, Deborah tells me, and brought the woman much peace.

Deborah's business partner, Chris Hotz, who plays Abraham Lincoln, Buster Brown, and most recently Wyatt Earp, is a skeptic.

When Deborah met Chris, he constantly teased her about being a "witch" or a "voodoo queen." Then, during their first season of historic walking tours, a ghostly visitor would not leave Deborah alone during one particular tour. Apparently "Al" had a relative on the tour and he wanted to give a message. Chris had noticed that she wasn't "quite right," and did most of the talking until the tour came to a rest spot. "Al" was so friendly and persistent, Deborah knew she had to share his message.

Deborah interrupted Chris. "There is a gentleman here, who calls himself Al, and he has recently passed. He said he walked with a temporary limp at the end of his life and he just wanted his children to know he is doing fine and Heaven is wonderful."

Chris looked at her and rolled his eyes, she says. No one on the tour said anything until after the tour was moving again, and a man approached Deborah and told her that Al was his father. At the end of the tour, he shared his story. He had lost his father a few months before, and Al told his son and daughter he would find a way to let them know that he had made it to Heaven and his opinion of the afterlife. Chris was amazed, but not ready to believe.

But, he knows of the intense research Deborah as done for all the tours and presentations, especially the Lincolns, including retracing the Lincolns' life in the south. He has witnessed numerous channeling sessions during ghost investigation, and he does believe she has a connection with Mary Lincoln. After each of these events, Chris respected he mediumship, the impressions from which he witnessed firsthand. As Chris says, "He may not believe so much in my mediumship...but he does believe in me."

Ghost Hunting

Deborah credits Janice Oberding (mentioned above) for her interest in paranormal investigations. She began attending conferences and investigations in Nevada, Oklahoma and Texas until she was able to develop her own business in Illinois. "I was hooked," she confesses. "I love working and living among the dead."

"Each investigation is its own unique experience," Deborah says. "I love working and living among the dead. Channeling has increased my fascination with ghost hunting. I have been pushed out of a cemetery (Virginia City), punched in the stomach (out West) and I have been kissed, hugged and touched; so physically those experiences are special.

"However my favorite investigations are the raw ones. I walk in, unfamiliar with the property, receive the medium impressions, confirm it with history and then go full circle as new information is found and confirmed. Our beloved hotel, The Phoenix-Mid-City Hotel, is a prime example, and the spirits just keep coming."

This hotel figures in one of Deborah's favorite stories on her Ghost Walk tour. When she and Chris first started the business in Bloomington, they had a storefront on Main Street. On the same block was a men's clothing store owned by Bill Fike. Bill told them about his great-uncle Ben Fike, who had been convicted of white slavery and kidnapping across state lines — he persuaded two women from Hannibal, Missouri, to follow him back to Bloomington for "hotel work." They were kept as hostages until one escaped, which eventually led to his conviction.

"The second year of our business, we added the hotel to the tour. It is deemed haunted by (paranormal researcher) John Zaffis. One evening, a group was communicating with pendulums and the name Ben came through. I then asked, 'Is this you, Ben Fike?' The pendulums went crazy and we all got cold, cold chills. My husband, Tom, immediately went through the hotel ledgers (we have most) and found his name! Yes, Ben Fike is still alive and 'operating' at our beloved historic hotel!"

She also loves working with newbies — first-timers — and loves to show them the ropes and is thrilled when they get it. Deborah sees ghost hunting as an awesome tool to connect history and mediumship. "Janice Oberding recently coined the term, 'historic ghost-investigator,' and that is exactly how I see my her role in a paranormal investigation."

Séances, Protection and Spirit Guides

Deborah does conduct séances. "During a séance I do enter a trance-like state," Deborah says. "Proper energy and keeping the channel open for communication is the key. I enjoy séances and realize through experience that energy balance is very important. Each séance is different, and the energy of the group determines my own actions. If I am in a 'safe' séance where there are people very close to me that I can trust, I am able to go into a deeper trance. However, if I am unfamiliar with the group members I am more cautious in my trance like state."

She do not use a "control," but believes protection is necessary. A prayer of protection is a must prior to her entering the room, she says, and also before the séance begins. She says she is then can surrender to the energy and allow the messages to flow direct from God's light through her. A control is a spirit that is well known to the medium, sometimes a relative, other times a spirit guide. This control acts as an intermediary between the medium and the spirit, and might convey their messages, thereby protecting the medium from direct contact with a spirit who might attempt to possess the medium.

Sometimes spirits channeled during a séance work through other attendees, rather than the medium. At a ghost conference in Virginia City, where part of the weekend included a séance,

Deborah received many messages including hearing from her step-grandmother Juanita (Nita).

Her cousin, Paula (also a medium) was there when Nita came was channeled through Janice Oberding and Butterfinger candy bars were flying around the room. Deborah says that later, through a private hypnotist hypnosis session, Nita's face appeared over Janice's face and smiled her special smile.

Janice's husband Bill was present and swore Nita, and not Janice, was present in the room. He was convinced that Janice was indeed taken over by this spirit.

Like the other psychics in this book, Deborah has her own spirit guides, but she has a different take on the subject than most.

"I was touched by Rosemary Altea's books and her channeling through her chief Native American (named Gray Eagle). As I read her book, I kept thinking, 'It's Jesus!' That night, I dreamed the chief's profile was being shown to me and as he turned his head towards me, his profile morphed into Jesus. He spoke to me and told me that all spirit guides are him. Each spirit guide has a purpose — short or long— to allow us to achieve our higher self and Jesus morphs himself to be that spirit to us. I have been blessed by many, for whatever purpose is upon me."

For Deborah's, her spirit guides include "Z," the a large and hilarious African American man from New Orleans, who reminds her through his antics not to take herself so seriously. He is also instrumental when dealing with missing people she is asked to find. She also has a Native American woman guide, who has grown up with her. Deborah first met her when they were both children. "When I first met her," she says, "she was a child and has grown with me. I actually met her once a few years back in Nevada. She continues to guide me and often appears in her 30's in my meditations. This represents the age I was when I became quite serious about developing my mediumship."

Family

Deborah says her husband, when they met, knew she was a little different. "Messages about business decisions and personal messages about family and my son are a part of my own personal decision making. My husband has always respected my 'opinions.' There were only a few times during our marriage that he Tom went against my intuition."

"Well, let's just say, my love and respect for him is more important! But I think, when I say no, he tends to think twice about a decision."

Deborah says that Tom doesn't necessarily believe in all that she "sees," but as she states lovingly, "He believes in me. He has met people as they leave a reading or a class and witnessed the change in their attitude and seen how my work fixed, encouraged, and enhanced their mental and physical state. Sometimes, he wished I would follow my own advice," she says, laughing.

Her son, Andrew, and his wife, Elayne, are aware of her abilities, but simply love her as "Oma" to their children, Sage and Brenna. "It is me they love and not my psychic abilities."

Deborah wants people to know that she is very human. "I am not reading your mind all the time, and, I am not the answer. God created the answers within each of us when we were created. Everyone is 'people like me'— God speaks to each of us."

Deborah can be reached by phone at 309-846-4306 or by email at ic_beyond@yahoo.com. Private readings and sessions are by appointment only.

Chapter 8
Mair MacKinnon

I met Mair MacKinnon when my massage therapist went on maternity leave. Jessica thought Mair and I would hit it off, and she was right. Mair and I became fast friends. She contributed a few stories to my ghost story book, lives in a haunted house, and employs the wisdom of those who have passed on to help her in her work as a massage therapist, naturopath, and homeopath.

Mair MacKinnon considers herself both a psychic and a sensitive, and feels the work she does requires those abilities. As a child, she became interested in all things psychic and otherworldly. "I bought witchcraft books and hid them under my bed, and would look for other things and order them through the mail, including a deck of Gypsy Fortune-Telling Cards when I was eleven," she says. "I then graduated to tarot cards. I never felt there was any thing woo-woo or weird about it. I always knew that I was getting the information from the universe — I didn't ever doubt that. I was getting what I was asking for." In addition to her therapeutic work, she also reads tarot cards.

Her strongest ability — which makes sense, given her job — is empathy. She has always believed in past lives, and is certain that what she does for a living is something she has done before — it has carried over to this lifetime. She finds it odd when people don't believe in psychic phenomena and things they can't see. "To me, the information is there for us; we have guides that are helping us. I have so many fabulous guides that are helping me, and I've always known it," she says.

Encounters with Spirits

The first time Mair saw a spirit was at her grandmother's house. Now, she laughs at her grandmother's reaction, but at the time, she was terrified. "It was the master bedroom at her house," she recalls. "I was probably eleven or twelve, and the room had been occupied by this old man that my grandmother had taken care of.

"My grandfather had died, and then she took in this old man. I don't know where he came from. It's so odd, now that I think back on it. Maybe she needed the money or something." She usually slept on the couch when she stayed over, but on this visit, her grandmother told her to take that bedroom. Mair didn't think anything of it …

"I'm in the bed and the door was closed," she continues. "My uncle, who lived in the house, was at work, and my grandmother was in another bedroom. I turned the light off to sleep, and I hear footsteps at the end of the bed! I turned the light on, and there's nothing there. So I shut the light back off, and footsteps again. I turn the light back on and I'm thinking, 'What the hell is that?' I shut off the light again, and somebody sat on the end of the bed! I turned the light back on and was thinking, 'This is really weird,' and I'm getting scared …

Mair saw that the bedroom door she had previously closed was open, because she could see the nightlight in the hall. She thought this was odd, but an even odder thing was about to happen: A big, tall figure emerged from behind the door, which opened against the wall. It stood in the doorway, looked at her, and then closed the door.

Mair turned the light on and yelled for her grandmother. "She's deaf as a post, and I'm saying, 'Oh my God, oh my God, oh my God,' and I lie there with the light on all night because I was afraid to get out of bed!

"As soon as it was light out, I got out of bed and ran into my grandmother's room. I'm hysterical and I wake her up. She puts her hearing aid in, and I tell her my story, and she said, "Oh, I know, honey. I've woken up in the morning and found black footprints across that bed!'"

These days, Mair has lost her fear of spirits. She lives in a Craftsman home in Alameda, Calif., which she shares with Henry, a ghost. And she's very happy he's around.

The first day she moved in, she saw him — a flash out of the corner of her eye — a person standing in the left-back corner of the living room. "I could feel him around," she says. "I didn't know his name at that point, so I started calling him George. I didn't see him for a while, but I knew he was there — I could still feel him."

She soon started working from home, and she could tell that "George" liked having her around. One day, she said, she heard a voice in her head say, "My name is Henry."

"It was weird," Mair relates. "I didn't hear an actual man's voice in the room, but I knew he had spoken, and his name is really Henry."

Others have seen Henry, including her friend Mary Lou, who described him as an older man, not very tall. "I would describe him as kind-looking," Mair says. "Not scary at all. No one has ever been scared by him. The feeling I have from just looking at him is that he is from the 1930s. Sandra, a psychic who was a client of mine, saw Henry and told me some things about him. She said that there was a ghost from the house behind us who was trying to invade this house, and Henry was protecting the house against this guy. She said this was good, because the guy was really creepy. I felt good hearing that."

Some time ago, her landlady was thinking of selling the house. Mair told her, "Oh, no, I can't do that, because Henry wouldn't like that," and told her about the ghost. The landlady said, "Oh, I know about him." Her daughter had lived in the house before Mair did. Mair says that Henry liked her and wouldn't like it if she moved, so that was that.

"Sometimes, Henry will open the doors," she says. "I think it was him who woke me up in the night once, when I might have been in danger. On that night, I was in bed asleep, and I'm kind of a light sleeper. The closet door has stuff in front of it so it won't open on its own. All of a sudden, in the middle of the night, I heard the creak, creak, creak of the hinges on the closet door trying to open. I sat up in bed, turned on the light, and looked. Nothing was there, of course. So, I thought, okay, and turned off the light. Creak, creak, creak started again right away, and I turned the light back on and I thought, 'All right, I got the message!'

"After that, I left the bedroom light on, turned on the kitchen light as well as some others, and stayed up about an hour. I think that there was someone prowling around the house, and Henry wanted me to turn the lights on. I heard no more creaking that night after I went back to bed. I think Henry was protecting me. I feel protected by him. Anyway, that's Henry. Good old Henry."

A psychic Mair sometimes visits told her she is surrounded by ghosts: "I see people who have ghosts around them, but the ghosts are usually of people who are related to them," the psychic said. "These spirits are not related to you. It is like you help them pass over."

Mair's Work, Her Guides, and Lessons Learned Through Reincarnation

Mair says she feels the spirits are helping her. "I know I'm not doing this work alone. I can feel them when I'm giving a massage, and also when I'm doing cranial and hypnosis work where I get into people's emotional states. I get a lot of help with that. I ask for help. And I'm very appreciative of it."

She is a doctor of naturopathic medicine, which uses complementary and alternative therapies to improve the body's ability to heal and maintain itself. There's an emphasis on a holistic approach, and natural methods are preferred to drugs.

Mair is also a homeopath. Homeopathy is a form of alternative medicine where patients are treated using highly diluted preparations of substances believed to cause healthy people to show symptoms of a disease or disorder, so it can be treated or cured, or are already proven herbal medicine.

In addition to examining the symptoms, homeopaths look at aspects of a patient's physical and psychological state and select a remedy based on all of the symptoms. Homeopathic medicine has a long history of curing chronic and acute health issues. It fell out of favor in the early 20th century, but there is a movement to bring it back to its former significance as a healing method.

While homeopathy is often regarded as controversial, I can attest that I've used it for pain of various kinds, allergies, stress, and menopausal symptoms, and found it to work as well or better than conventional medicine and with fewer side effects.

As Mair describes her practice, "I use all forms of natural medicine to educate and enhance the quality of the lives of my clients." She has worked in this field for more than 24 years, and offers a variety of healing methods that include craniosacral therapy, therapeutic massage full-spectrum and laser light therapy, clinical hypnotherapy, homeopathy, and nutritional counseling.

Mair's patients speak often of how intuitively she deals with their problems. Some of that is part of who she is. But who Mair is she became in large part to her guides. And what she does, she owes in part to them, her own intuition, a bizarre series of circumstances, and to a psychic named Anna Franz.

"I went to this psychic when I was 18, and it was this little old lady just sitting in her kitchen," Mair told me. "Her name was Anna Franz. I'll never forget her. I can't remember where I heard about her, but my friend Kathy and I called her and made an appointment, and you went to her house. She didn't charge you — you could just give her a donation.

"When she started talking to me, and when she talked to Kathy, she was really right on. But the thing she really emphasized with me were the guides.. She said, 'You know, you really have very strong guides around you, and you are going to be doing healing work, and they are going to help you.'

"I was working for Kaiser as a lab tech, and I thought that was what she meant (laughs) but that wasn't it. Not even."

Anna told Mair that some of the help the guides offer would come from an unexpected source. "The first thing she said to me was … it's funny, I still remember everything, even though I was only 18. It was so huge for me, this reading. I've had lots of readings since then that I couldn't tell you what they said to save my life, but she really had a huge impact.

"She said, 'I see something about your mother's heart." I said, 'Well, that's funny, because today my mother had an EKG." It was Mair's adopted mother, but the psychic didn't know that. Later in the reading, Anna told her that she was getting a strong message from the other side. "She told me," Mair says, "that the message was from my mother, but that didn't make sense to her 'I'm going to give you the message and you can make of it what you will,' Anna told me.

"So she tells me that my mother said that she's looking out for me and is proud of me and wants to help me, and she's always there for me, etc. And the psychic still doesn't understand this. And I said, 'I'm adopted.' And she said, 'Ah, well, apparently your mother has passed over—your birth mother.'"

Mair had no idea her birth mother had died, but she didn't doubt it. "And, in fact, since then, I've seen my mother in spirit. She's come. She came in a craniosacral session, and I know she's with me often."

Anna then talked about the other guides helping Mair. "I have a strong Native American guide, and a wizard guide, and she described these people who were around me and would be helping me."

The way Mair moved on from her traditional laboratory job for Kaiser into alternative medicine was no less odd. "It was funny: everything changed because I had a two serious car accidents. I knew I wasn't supposed to be working in the lab at Kaiser, but I didn't know what I was supposed to be doing. Then, I had a car accident, and I was off work for a few months. And during that time I started reading all the Edgar Cayce material." Edgar Cayce, known as the "sleeping prophet," was a psychic who conveyed information on subjects including healing, Atlantis, and reincarnation while in a trance. "And I kept thinking, 'I know this isn't the right job for me, and I know I hate it there and I want out and I'm not contributing and it's just paying the bills.'"

The following year, she had another car accident, this one worse than the first. It was 1:30 a.m. and Mair had just gotten off work at the lab. Someone driving a dark-brown truck had stopped on the freeway in the fast lane, turned sideways, and turned his lights off. Mair ran right into him in her car. "And after that happened, he pulled off the road, and put his flashers on, was waving a flashlight, so when the cops got there, he pretended he always had been doing that."

The cops originally had blamed Mair for causing the accident, but an EMT, who had seen the entire accident, came to her rescue. "He got me out of the car, carried me across the freeway, the ambulance comes, and I'm laying in the ambulance thinking, 'Okay, I guess I got the message!'"

But she still wasn't sure it was time to leave her dull night job and become herself. She was off work for a year recovering from the accident, and as part of her physical therapy, saw a chiropractor. She and Mair became friends. "She wanted me to go to this raw foods and wheatgrass juice convention in San Diego. She also said, 'I think you should go to massage school.' At the time, I thought, 'I can't even move, how can I do massage?' and I didn't like massage. I didn't like to give it, I didn't like to get massages.

"But I went to this thing in San Diego. I was on disability, and couldn't afford a hotel, so I stayed in a dorm. It was three people to a room. One other bed was filled with this woman from Alaska and the other bed changed every week. I stayed there three weeks, and so did Barbara, the woman in the other bed. It was always a massage therapist that filled the third bed! How many times did I have to get hit over the head that what I was doing needed to change?"

Mair went to massage school and it transformed her life. She realized she was good at it, and it was revelatory. After she started working for the chiropractor her then-husband once worked for, she realized that this was more than just massage. It was a deeper connection with people than she ever had before. She started studying everything she could — every kind of bodywork. She went to hypnotherapy school and became a clinical hypnotherapist, and made a serious study of herbology, which she had been interested in since she was a teenager. Then, Mair tells me, she met someone who played a pivotal part in her life, and continues to do so.

"I had this mentor, a physical therapist named Don Schwartz. He was blind, but was the most phenomenal healer. Before I ever went to massage school, I went to career counseling, and the woman who was the career counselor was his wife. We became very good friends, and I became really close to him. And every time I would go to his house, he would teach me something else. When he died, his wife, Mary Lou, and I had a falling-out and that was it. I never saw her again, never went to the house. It was like it was all about him. It was all about his connection with him. I needed him in my life. And he is one of my guides."

As for her other spirit guides — "There's this big bear that's there with me. He's there a lot; he's very human to me. But, he's a bear, a bear shape. I've seen him in meditation and hypnosis. I've seen the other guides, too. When I was in hypnosis school, I got in touch with that.

"There's an old woman, but I don't know who that is. I don't think it is my mother, because my mother was young when she died. I don't know how many guides I have. Every now and then I'll glimpse something in my mind. But I know I've done this work for many lifetimes, and I think we carry forward people who worked with you before. I was a Native American medicine woman. I was a veterinarian in Scotland, and I know I've been a witch. I know these have been lifetimes I've lived."

Mair says she has known from a young age that she's been here before. She was kicked out of Catholic catechism classes when she was ten years old for talking to her classmates about reincarnation.

Mair was adopted before birth, and knew from the get-go because her adoptive mother told her. She said she better understands her relationship with her adoptive mother after past-life regression showed her how they related to each other in those past lives. She said her grandmother, who treated her as her favorite grandchild, had treated her that way before: "She was my nanny in another life. I was actually a prince and she was my nanny. And my mother was her real son. I was the favorite."

Except for Don and her mother, Mair has no sense of knowing any of her other guides in past or current lifetimes, but she knows they are there. "I ask for help," she says. "I know that Merlin is one of my guides that's come to me again and again. And my Native American guide, I think his name is something Eagle. I really connect with the eagle part. It's something like Running Eagle, which is weird, since eagles aren't exactly known for their running!

"And I know I have other people who are there with me, but I believe in God, and to me, God is the goddess or the universe. God is not this guy who is here, but is the force of the universe. And I think these guides are all part of that, and we're all connected, and that's what the God connection is, no matter what plane you're on. That we're all here to do the work that we're here to do and we're helping each other and we're interconnected in an interdependent kind of way."

Sometimes, she says, she will be in a session with someone and won't know how to help them. So she connects with her guides, saying to them, "You're always here helping me, so please help me because I don't know what to do.' And immediately, it comes, and I never worry that I'm not going to know how to treat someone, because I'm never alone with it."

Mair describes it as not like a voice, but more a "knowing." It doesn't always come from the same guide; people bring their own guides, and she depends on that as well. She thinks everyone's guide or guides will come in with them and they will know what that person needs. "From the minute the patient walks in the door, I have my radar on. And that radar is helped by these other entities."

Keeping Things Clear, Clean, and Separate

Mair's work involves energy — from plants, light, the universe, and the people who are her patients. This energy can be good, but it can be bad as well.

"I do cleansing rituals," she says. "Some people who come in, I really have to cleanse when they leave. I have to sage and salt, really go around and get everything out. There are people who come in who might be toxic — we all meet those people. I feel like I can just let it go. I feel like I have an evil eye on the front door— okay, leave your stuff at the door. I don't feel like I absorb negative energy."

Separating her own emotions from those of the people she is treating is essential to her own well-being. I can attest that a lot of emotions come to the surface during a craniosacral therapy session, and it can be tricky for practitioners to let go of what they are absorbing emotionally. "When I do craniosacral work on somebody, I know information is going to come to me, and I know I don't have to hang on to that," Mair says. "I know I'm going to feel things, I'm going to get the info in my head, and I'm going to feel emotional and I'm going to feel pain and it's going to pass, because it's not about me. … I'm really clear about that. And I think that's something some practitioners can't do — to let go. I do need time to recharge; I do need to be alone a lot to recharge. I would get burned out if I didn't have a lot of time to myself."

Sometimes there is clearing work to be done on the psychic level as well. Mair recalls that the angel Gabriel once appeared to her. It was during a particularly difficult relationship, and she was having a tough time. She had gone to hypnosis school and past-life regression, and knew there were a lot of issues between them.

"But then I found out his ex-girlfriend had gone to this black magician and put a curse on me. It was ugly and all kinds of bad things were happening and I didn't know why, and then I found out that was why."

One morning Mair woke up out of a sound sleep and saw an angel at the end of her bed. The angel told her that he was Gabriel and that she needed to let go of her fear and everything would be fine. Mair couldn't speak, and the angel disappeared. "It still sends shivers down my spine to think about it," she says. I asked myself, 'Did that just happen?' I don't tell many people about it because they think I'm crazy. "For days, I was walking around wondering about what happened. Even now, when I look back on it, it's like it was a shock to my system. It was incredible. And I am so grateful because it was just what I needed at the time. It was a life-changing experience."

Being Mair and Advice for Others

"I feel like I've been reincarnated a lot," Mair says. "I feel like I've been around the block a few times, and I feel like my acuity about things is pretty good. Not always about myself, but about what's happening with other people. I feel I have a job to do, and my job is to be a kind of balancing force for what's happening with people's health. I think it's mostly about health for me, I think that's my job here, and I accept it."

Mair says it's very frustrating to her when she knows something that will help somebody and they choose to do something else.

"But it's their path, and I know that, so I can let that go, and say 'Okay, I'm here, I'm doing my job, I'm available if they get a message that their choice is not right."

And for Mair, having unusual abilities is *her* path to walk: "You just have to do what you have to do and not expect that everyone is going to honor that. If you're outside of the norm, you're not going to ever be accepted by the majority of the people.

"When I start to get frustrated, I think, 'I can't be upset at them.' They can't tell – they aren't doing this on purpose, they can't tell. It releases me from any judgment I have about them. They are who they are, and they can't do anything about that, just like me."

You can reach Mair through her website http://web.me.com/mairmackinnon/www.mairmackinnon.com/Welcome.html

Chapter 9
Gypse Jacquaar

I met Gypse Jacquaar when I advertised for a Tarot reader to do readings every other Sunday in my bookstore. We've since become great friends. For this book, she doesn't want her real name used, so Gypse she shall be. I didn't know her real name for months after I met her. Gypse suits her. She is a free spirit, unafraid to be who she is.

She spends a lot of time exploring the Tarot and the more arcane areas of spirituality, with personal growth for herself and others as her focus. She says she remembers me from a previous life, when we were Gypsies together in France. She guides her work and personal life by message from spirits and the Tarot. While on the earthly plane, she owns and operates a business that provides computer-aided design (CAD) for architects, engineers, and contractors.

Gypse Jacqaar grew up in upstate New York, the daughter of scientists. There were no psychics in her family, but she credits her parents with giving her a good grounding for investigation. Although they were not into the occult, they liked learning and intellectual exploration.

Today, Gypse uses her communication with advanced spirits to guide her life and her business.

"I started as a medium with spirits who had been incarnated as human beings, and I wouldn't say they were extremely enlightened," she says. "They were human beings who had psychic abilities and knew how to communicate with people who are still here."

Her foray into the world of spirit began when she was a freshman in high school. Her mother was an alcoholic, and the teenager struggled for a way to cope.

"I don't even remember where I heard about automatic writing," she says. "I think I read a book about a psychic or someone who talked with the spirits, and from that book, I realized spirit communication was possible."

The messages Gypse received via automatic writing explained to her why her mother was an alcoholic, how to deal with it, and showed her that there was more to life than what she was experiencing on the physical plane. They also told her that there are such things as spirit guides. In fact, the messages told her, the spirits who came through via automatic writing *were* her guides.

"I want to stress that people receive and transmit psychic information in different ways, and I was very gifted verbally," Gypse says. "I had a high IQ for writing and reading, so it was natural for me to do automatic writing as a way for my psychic ability to manifest itself."

She receives information verbally in her head, and she's noticed over the years that people who are psychic receive information very differently. Some say that things fall off the wall, or lights go on and off. "I will get a message verbally — 'I'm a ghost, I'm here.' I might get a message telepathically. And I notice, for me, the spirit might not even be speaking English, but the message will still come through in fairly articulate terms."

The teenage Gypse kept her automatic writing notebook in a drawer, and in writing, something psychically opened up in her, and when she went to college, she felt very strongly that she had to go to one particular school. When she got there, she found out it was very haunted.

Early Mediumistic Experiences

Gypse attended Wells College in Aurora, New York. There are many stories of campus hauntings, including that of Max, the spirit who came through to her during several séances in dark dorm rooms.

According to Gypse, Max was a security guard who perished in a fire while rescuing some girls trapped in a campus building that stood where Morgan Hall now stands - it houses the art department. Perhaps Max communicated through Gypse because she was an art history major and spent a lot of time in Morgan Hall? A spirit claiming to be a music professor also made himself known at the séances she conducted.

Studying with the Witches

After college, Gypse threw herself into the world of art and artists, which taught her to see life much differently than her conservative upbringing had taught her. And, in that world, she met her husband, whom she describes as "crazy, and really, really open."

It was after getting married that Gypse decided to study witchcraft. She took a course from the "Witches of New Bern," Gavin and Yvonne Frost. If you ever read any comic books as a kid, back there among the ads for magic tricks and black soap, was one proclaiming "Learn to Be a Witch!" Writing to the address therein introduced you to Gavin and Yvonne, and the Church and School of Wicca. Taught by correspondence, you could (and still can) learn about developing psychic power, telepathy, psychic healing, herbs, and reincarnation, among other esoterica in the Essential Witchcraft course.

The course opened Gypse up more than she could handle, in the psychic sense, and she kept having strange and unsettling experiences, so she never finished the course.

Those witches are fantastic," she says. "They did an astral course and were working with students on the astral plane. It was very easy for me to go out on the astral at the time. Unfortunately, I found this ability is one thing that goes away with age. The astral is where you get a lot of your best training (from discarnate entities and people traveling by astral projection) — you get to talk with those who were and are psychics and others with great knowledge. I learned that from Gavin and Yvonne Frost."

Gypse said she had to learn to pay attention to supernatural things that seem mundane now, because they happen so often but were very important to her personal growth. "It was a correspondence course. It just opened me up to the fact that there is a whole different system, and one thing the witches impressed upon me was that their course was very rigorous and there was a lot of responsibility.

"You weren't just running around doing spells — you did a lot of research. They emphasized that you are on your own and you make your own life. That really impressed me."

Communing with the Spirits

Gypse believes everyone has spirits at different levels of evolution. You might have your family, your grandparents, etc. Some people in your family might contact you, but they are still at the same level of enlightenment they were when they died, and trying to solve their own karmic problems — they are not enlightened. The spirits she communicates with are by and large not her own ancestors, although her grandmother, who was from the Scottish highlands, sometimes pops in for a visit. Her grandmother read tea leaves, but had no interest in the occult — to read tea leaves was normal in her culture, and many people did so.

"If you keep working, you have angels around you, you have gods and goddesses around you, and you have more enlightened spirits around you, like spiritual masters," Gypse says. "You have a hierarchy of spirits around you, and then you have your highest spirit, whatever it is that you believe — god, goddess, Jesus, Isis, whomever."

Gypse can see those spirits and communicate with them. "Sometimes I see them walking around and usually, 90 percent of the time, I see them as a shadowy form in my own mind, but I can describe very clearly what they look like and what they have on and they talk to me," she says. "And they talk to me constantly." They'll talk to her in the morning, when she reads her Tarot cards, and tell her what her daily "assignments" are, and she always writes them down. Some days, she says, the spirit messages come every few hours and she ends up with stacks and stacks of notes.

"At this point, I am doing this note writing as a meditation and have learned to just start crossing things off. Going back, some years the spirits were really accurate and other years, they were not so accurate because I wasn't really able to take in what they were saying. I was too worried about me." Sometimes, she says, what she thinks is significant is not validated by spirit message.

In Gypse's world, spirits are not ghosts. Ghosts are spirits who are not evolving. The spirits she sees are evolving in the spirit world. She doesn't like the word "guide," but uses it because it's easily understandable by others.

Gypse's guides are strict, and let her know what she can and cannot reveal about her spiritual life. One of her spirit guides, the only one she was free to talk about , is a fakir, a Muslim or Hindu monk said to be a wonder worker. "She likes to move things around," Gypse says. "She's very advanced — she's a witch — she was an aristocrat in England. So she just does that. She is at a very high level, but she can't stop doing that. She enjoys doing it and she does it for fun."

Gypse went into computer drafting because she was interested in art. "I had spirits around me who were interested in that, were interested in the computers, were interested in working in that industry in the spirit world, and interested in furthering technology and helping mankind by furthering technology and so they have directed me in this company."

Have you ever wondered why you end up doing certain things, make your living a certain way? Gypse believes that this is all the work of the enlightened spirits.

"They tell me what to do. You can say my boss is the highest force and then there are others on the lower scale, down where we are, and they have different things they want me to accomplish, so the company is run by them in the spirit world and me on the earth plane.

"So, it's coming through me in my work, and, actually I'm a CEO, but the spirits are like my board of directors," Gypse says. "They are all advising me, and sometimes it's hard to figure out what they are saying because I have so many spirits telling me so many things. I have to sift through and decide which spirit to listen to now, which spirit to listen to next week."

Gypse rarely encounters malevolent spirits. She recalls one incident when she was working on a now-defunct website that gave automatic Tarot readings.

"It got taken over by Satanism, and I couldn't figure out why. The guy who wrote the site for me told me later that his ex-girlfriend was into the dark side of Santeria. I can never use the code or the site again, because very time I try to use it, I see the Devil. So, that's a malevolent spirit.

"I think the problem is that I can't see the bad in people," she continues. "I can't see it, so I'm in danger. I have to wait for the spirits to come and tell me and sometimes the spirits will make me do something —interact and then I find out that person is going to do me in and that's my weak spot. I can't see. I'm more of an optimist."

Her Spirit Family

Gypse doesn't work with her ancestors — not her blood ancestors, at any rate. She works with a family she has found in the spirit world. But sometimes the lines are blurred. Her grandfather (who came to her in spirit) claimed that he knows someone she knows in this life, and had a message. "So, I told this person that I got a certain message from my grandfather. He understood it and was able to interpret it and help me with it, and it was really strange."

Gypse says she has a spirit daughter who is in pre-med. "My aunt was married to a professor at Harvard medical school. He died. My aunt had just had a brain tumor removed, noncancerous, and my spirit daughter assisted in the surgery — I didn't tell my aunt this. This is how the spirits help us. And then I got freaked out, because my uncle, when he was alive, was really terrifying, he was a snob. When you think of a superstar doctor, that's him.

"All of a sudden, I hear him saying that my spirit daughter is phenomenal, that he wants to train her to become a surgeon. Well, she wasn't planning on becoming a surgeon. In my mind, she is my daughter. My spirit family is in a different world, and I am very close to her.

"When they suddenly cross the line, and someone peripheral to my real family that I barely know, is suddenly directing my spirit child, I can't explain how strange it is. Because the message coming through was so strong. I guess somewhere in the spirit world my ancestors are connected to my sprit family and we all knew each other and we're all going to reincarnate again.

"Maybe part of me thinks this world isn't really real, it's all happening in the spirit world, and when they start interpenetrating with my real family who are dead, my brain can barely handle it. Because there's a difference in my mind, between my spirit family, who doesn't feel like they are dead to me, and my uncle, who I know died. And if I hear him, he's faint, and I'm not hanging out with him in the spirit plane, I never heard from him after he died.

"So, I'm thinking, 'What does this mean?' I'm growing in my understanding of how the spirits relate. Both these incidents show me I don't control this. I'm just watching this. I'm getting the messages. They don't have anything to do with me. It very much disturbs me. It's a different aspect of the sprit world that I'm not used to.

"Life is bigger than us. The abilities I have are not necessarily for me, but I can observe more, but I don't always know what it means, I just know it is happening.

"I was so disturbed. What I wanted to be able to do is to call my aunt and say my daughter is working with your husband. That's where the disconnect is. She would say, but my husband is dead, and you don't have a daughter. You better go see a shrink!"

Gypse thinks her uncle came to her because he wants her spirit daughter to be a surgeon. She was going to be a dermatologist. "In another life, I will have children. He's telling me not to hold my future child back, he wants her to go to medical school to become a surgeon. And to most people walking around, I have no daughter; it's just me. But I know I have a daughter. It's like I see you with your spirit daughter. I know you have a spirit child. When that child comes to me, I give you the message. I feel like I know that child."

The spirit world is very, very real, she says. In some ways, more real to her than this everyday world. "I feel more comfortable with people who are dead than alive, the people who have crossed over. The people who are alive, they are going to go elsewhere. The people who are over there, I feel more solid with that."

Art Imitates Life

Gypse describes an episode from the first season of the television show Six Feet Under that she says fairly accurately depicts what she experiences. David, one of the mortician characters, is working on the body of a gang leader. Meanwhile, the spirit of the dead man is standing next to David, giving him life advice.

The dead man, "Hangs out with David and helps him get tough," Gypse says. "It's not anything scary, and what's implied, and what's so accurate is, if you experience it, it's that normal, once you get used to it."

"There's the feeling that the spirit giving the advice is somehow wiser, and can see more — what you can't see, and you see David's willingness to listen to the advice. And it's perfect, because he's using it at work, he's using it at his job. Whoever wrote that really knows what it's like. It's a fictional story, but the way it's portrayed is not fictional, it really is like that," she says.

"I would say to people who haven't experienced it, that it's a really accurate depiction. This is how I live, that's how I do my job."

The Tarot

Gypse views the Tarot as a sacred text like the Bible or other historic spiritual record. She was drawn to the cards, she thinks, because of her art background. She equates studying the Tarot with the study of the Torah — one of her grandfathers was Jewish. Both, she says, are an ongoing study of self-analysis and self-understanding of your spiritual path.

"I find that when you go to church and you read the Bible, it's different. You're praying, you're interacting with Jesus. When you are a witch, you're creating your reality with your meditation, your psychic protections, your spirits, and your spells" she says. "And when you do the Tarot, it's almost like you're doing surgery on your inner self, because you realize you're going to become enlightened and it's a process you work on every day."

She reads the Tarot a couple of hours a day, and says that she's recently begun receiving messages from God, *telling* her to continue to read the Tarot. While Gypse believes in Jesus, she does not consider herself a Christian, because she also believes that other deities exist. "What's hilarious is that my sister is in the Christian Right, and I had a question about something and she asked me why I didn't open the Bible at random and see what it has to say (this is called stichomancy). I mean, really, what's the difference between opening the Bible and using the Tarot?"

Whether she's reading for herself or for others, she sometimes gets messages for which the meaning isn't known.

"I think is was last Friday. I was throwing the cards. I had decided to throw the cards for morning, noon, afternoon, and evening, just to see what's happening. I got the Devil at noon," she says. The Devil card is said to mean excess or loss of control. "What does that mean? It had no meaning in my current life. Well, at noon, I was sitting there paying some bills and there were all these sirens. There was a big fire and a house burnt down, the fire was out of control. It's just information. Is that what the card meant? Who knows? It's just a reminder to be alert."

When Gypse was reading Tarot cards in my store, she had many repeat customers who found her to be very accurate. But she remembers few of those readings, as she enters an altered state when doing them. "They aren't about me," she said. "The messages I get are for the person I'm reading for — I don't feel that I'm supposed to remember them."

She reminded me that she saw my partner in my cards. "He was the Six of Cups. I told you that would have a relationship with a soul mate and you already had met him."

Like other psychics in this book, Gypse says people often don't hear messages if they are not ready to hear them. If they come for a reading on one thing, they won't listen to messages about something else. It's where the person being read is focused — if they want information on a current situation, they aren't interested in what might happen in the future.

When I was looking for psychics to interview, I asked a woman I know who is active in the local Tarot community. She told me that she isn't psychic. I also read Tarot cards, but I am not psychic. I know what the cards mean and how they relate to each other in a layout, but I rarely feel comfortable reading for other people.

I asked Gypse how people who aren't psychic get messages to pass along to people. Gypse feels reading Tarot cards, even just for yourself, opens you up to other spiritual knowledge; that this knowledge comes from a part of our brain we don't use, but did use in ancient times.

"It's using your brain, it's increasing your awareness. You're talking to me now, and I have limitations in my awareness. If I were the Dalai Lama, I would be telling you very different things. The spiritual world exists. Man is evolving and one day, the word psychic won't exist. We think, in this modern culture, that we are so advanced. I think we are primitive and just not using parts of our brain. Some cultures are very comfortable using that part of our brain — Native Americans and others."

She said that if people used that part of their brain, they would tune in to the spiritual side of life. "I was reading something by Malidoma Somé. He is a shaman in West Africa. He's pretty radical. He says that in his culture, they respect the earth, and that's the first thing. And they develop their psychic skills based on that."

The way we view reality governs how we behave, she says. In her case, she works both ways — she has what people would consider "normal" periods and then she goes into another level of awareness. To her, it's normal, because she is used to herself — to having experiences and having spirits come and tell her how to interpret these experiences and tell her what to do.

Here's a case in point, with the spirits speaking through the Tarot: "The other day I had to go into a phone conference and I looked at the cards before I went into the meeting, I had one engineer working with me. We had written two kinds of proposals — I saw in the cards that the client was interested in developing the secondary proposal. I saw they had money for that, not the first proposal. I mentioned this to the engineer before we went into the meeting, and he wondered how I knew that.

"I just told him, 'Look, I read it in the Tarot cards,' and he looked at me and said 'Okay.' Why should I be ashamed of this? I'm tired of pretending I don't read the Tarot cards."

She said she doesn't always know how to interpret the cards — that they serve as more of an analysis tool. "You have to figure out how to look at yourself and where your strengths and weaknesses lie. It's not predictions, it's more like the trends. It's like the weather. What are the odds? What's that person's temperament? What's my karma? Then make a more educated guess."

Most Tarot readers will tell you that the cards show what will happen if you continue on the path you are on. Change your path, change your life.

I mentioned that some people say you can't read your own Tarot cards because you will just project onto the cards what you want them to say.

Gypse strongly disagrees. "That is completely wrong," she says. "You can give yourself total therapy with the cards. I've been reading the cards for years, and I know where I am with my life's journey with the cards and what my current challenges are, based on the iconography of the cards. You have certain tests you have to go through, you have certain challenges that you cannot escape as a growing soul. So the cards tell you what you have to learn, and what you need to work on. They are very humbling. It's a good way to look at yourself and see your bad side. It's not so clear when I see my good side – 'Okay, so I'm doing well, but I'm still gong to have problems. I'm glad I'm doing well here, now I'm going to have to learn this…'"

Relationships on the Earth Plane

Gypse is still married to the "crazy artist" she met shortly after college. She says she's always giving him messages. "He's used to it. I tell him the spirits say we should be doing this and the spirits say we should be doing that. And he'll ask me, 'What are the sprits saying now?' and sometimes he just ignores me.

"He's very supportive. He thinks the messages are accurate. I give him a lot of credit to be able to grow with the messages because I've given him some really hard ones."

She's had people she's given messages to get really angry with her, because she's telling them what they don't want to do, but really should be doing. The messages could have to do with anything from changing jobs to divorcing a spouse to whether to have a child, to more mundane matters in everyday life.

"It is kind of an invasion of space. It's kind of rude. I'm very unaware in that way. I'm a clunky Taurus. I'm not the most diplomatic person, and some people take it the wrong way."

Her parents, she said, believe in her abilities because they've been helped by them. With other people, she's usually open. Sometimes too open, she said. "Because I assume people know what I'm talking about. If I remember someone from another life, like I remember you, I tell them. Most people don't remember; I don't know why."

Spirits Can Be Tough Taskmasters

Gypse says the spirit world has laws. She can't talk about some things. "I don't even know why. All I know is that bad things happen when I talk too much. There's some kind of energy released and it's dangerous." The spirits, in fact, told her that she could not use her real name for this book.

There are laws of the universe, she said. Laws of nature. The amount of our brain we use isn't much. We aren't trained to use our subconscious, she believes. This belief is shared by parts of the psychoanalytic community, that there are inner forces (our subconscious) that effect our external behavior.

When she did readings in a room in my bookstore, she was very particular about what was in the room. Things were removed, and other things were taken in. Sometimes, she would bring things with her — a statue, a flower, a candle. "I'm always like that," she said. "Because when you change things around, you change the energy and the dynamic. I had to set up my space so the spirits could come and help me.

"Sometimes, I bring a thing something home and it sits at the bottom of the stairs. Someone might give me a present and it might sit at the bottom of the stairs for a year. The spirits have to tell me what to do with it."

In daily life and work, Gypse is striving to find balance. "I'm more on the spiritual plane, but I'm trying to learn how to take the messages and make them manifest in positive ways. That's my current task."

Chapter 10
You *Can* Try This At Home

As some of the psychics have mentioned, things like tarot cards are simply ways to focus the mind and receive the messages, wherever they may come from. Here are some psychic exercises you can do at home. Most of these techniques are based on personal experience:

Scrying – Scrying involves seeing things psychically in a medium, for obtaining spiritual visions. Some use a crystal ball, water in a black bowl, a black mirror, or just an every-day mirror.

How to Scry Using an Ordinary Mirror

What you'll need:

A mirror, preferably in a spot you can sit or kneel in front of and be comfortable

A flashlight or a candle

The Process:

- Find a location where you aren't likely to be disturbed.
- Turn off all the lights.
- Light your candle or prepare your flashlight
- Sit in front of the mirror. Close your eyes and pray or meditate, visualizing a bright, white light of protection coming from above to surround you.
- When you're ready, open your eyes and pick up your candle or flashlight
- Gaze into the mirror and hold the candle or flashlight a few inches below your face. Allow your eyes to go out of focus.

• Relax and open your mind, and images should appear in the mirror. They might be hazy. In fact, your own face, should you look at it, should be hazy, because you are so relaxed and your eyes are out of focus.

• If you look to your right, you might see your spirit guide.

• If you look to your left, you might see a departed loved one.

If you like, ask questions in your mind as you gaze. Images should appear that give you clues to the answers. You can also keep your mind blank and see what messages come through on their own. Don't perform scrying for more than 20 minutes or so the first, as it can be tiring ; you can increase increase the time as you gain experience. After each session, write down what you saw.

A black scrying mirror. Created by using black spray paint on a pane of glass from the hardware store.

How to Read Tea Leaves

The art of reading tea leaves is called tasseography.

This is fun to do with a friend, sitting around a table on a Sunday afternoon, deciphering the messages in each other's cups!

What You'll Need

A white cup with no designs on the inside
A saucer or small plate
Loose tea

The Process:

• Prepare a cup of tea with loose tea leaves. Put the normal amount of leaves into the cup, with no tea ball or strainer.

• Drink the tea, leaving a very small amount of liquid at the bottom of the cup.

• Hold the cup in your left hand, and slowly swirl the contents three times clockwise. Try to make sure that the leaves are moved towards the rim of the cup.

• Place the cup upside down on the saucer, holding it there for seven seconds while letting the fluids drain.

• Turn the tea cup right side up again, the handle should face the reader while he or she interprets the symbols and images.

Interpretations:

• Many leaves point to a full life.

• Lots of specific images symbolize many important issues in the person's life.

• Contradicting images imply indecision.

• The larger images are the more important issues in the person's life.

• Objects on the left of the handle may denote the past, and objects to the right may be in the future.

• It is believed that symbols near the rim of the tea cup refer to the present or the near future, while those towards the bottom of the cup are seen as the past.

These are only guidelines to help you get started. A genuine reading is dependent upon the reader's interpretation of the symbols.

To find a list of some of the more common symbols you'll see and their traditional meanings, visit Tea Leaves Meaning (http://tealeavesmeaning.blogspot.com/2009/06/tea-leaf-symbols-meanings.html). There are books and websites that offer more detailed information.

Make tea with the leaves loose in the cup.

Drink most of the tea, leaving just a bit of liquid.

Turn the cup over on the saucer. Read the leaves that are left in the cup.

Using a Pendulum to Contact Spirits and Receive Messages

Using a pendulum is a form of dowsing, — a type of divination used not only for spirit communication, but also to find water, buried metals, lost objects, oil, or grave sites, or other objects.

What You'll Need:

You can use almost anything as a pendulum on a thread, string, or chain; a needle at the end of an eight-inch piece of thread, a pendant necklace, or a rock tied to a piece of string. If you're using thread or string, it's helpful to tie a knot at the top to give yourself something to grip.

If you choose to buy a pendulum at a metaphysical store, look for the one that "speaks" to you. You'll know exactly what I mean when you find it.

Do not let anyone else use your pendulum – it's thought that they absorb energy, and you want to keep your pendulum attuned to you.

The Process:

• Pray or meditate, and envision yourself surrounded by a protective circle of white light.

• When you have centered yourself, take hold of the end of the string, thread, or chain with your thumb and first finger. Let the pendulum swing freely.

•Hold the pendulum in front of you.

• If you have trouble keeping your arm steady, you can brace it with your other hand by holding your forearm just below the elbow. You can also rest the elbow of your pendulum arm on a table, as long as the pendulum can still swing freely.

• First, you'll want to figure out which movement indicates a positive answer. Let the pendulum hang freely and keep your eyes focused on the rock, or pendant. When you're ready, ask the pendulum, "Show me 'Yes.'" It will swing in one direction. It could swing back and forth, front to back, or rotate in a circle clockwise or counter clockwise.

• Perform the same operation, this time asking the pendulum to "Show me 'No.'"

• Now, you're ready to ask questions. All questions need to be phrased so that the answers are "yes" or "no." If a spirit is not present, or does not want to answer the question, the pendulum will remain still.

• First, ask the spirit for permission to ask questions. If the pendulum swings in the direction of yes, you may go ahead. If it swings in the direction of "no," this isn't a good time to ask.

• If you have attempted to contact a specific spirit, and you receive a "no" when asking permission, try someone else.

• Sometimes the pendulum will swing wildly. I always interpret this as meaning the spirit is present and, wants you to know it's present, but doesn't want to communicate through the pendulum.

• When you have decided to stop using the pendulum, thank all the spirits who have come through for their cooperation and ask them to leave at this time.

You can also use the pendulum like a Ouija board, by drawing letters on a piece of paper and hanging it over the paper while asking questions.

Glossary

Alchemy — A precursor to Pre-dates chemistry that originated in medieval times, based on a theory of the transformation of matter, and originated in Medieval times. It's based on a theory of the transformation of matter. Many alchemists attempted to convert base metals into gold, or find a universal elixir (one that would benefit everyone).

Angel of Death — In the Christian Bible, Azrael, is the personification of death.

Apparition — A supernatural manifestation of a deceased person
or animal; ghost, spirit, or specter.

Apport — The paranormal transference of something an article from one place to another, or the appearance of an article from an unknown source. This phenomena often is often associated with poltergeist activity or séances.

Astral Projection — Also known as "out of body experience". It is believed to result when the astral body, or spirit, separates from the physical body.

Botanica — A Botanica is a retail store that sells folk medicine, religious candles and statuary, amulets, and other products regarded as magical, primarily catering to those who participate in the magical practices/ and/or religions of Santeria or Yoruba.

Discarnate — Has no physical form or body.

Electronic Voice Phenomena (EVP) – Sounds or voices recorded which that are heard only upon playback. Discovered by Konstantin Raudive. Usually recorded found in a range from 0 to– 300 Hz (human speech is generally within 500— and 2000 Hz, and has never been recorded below 300 Hz).

Extra-Sensory sensory Perception (ESP) — Communication or perception by means other than the physical senses.

Ghost — The disembodied spirit or image of a dead person. Ghosts are the most common of the paranormal phenomena.

Haunting — Paranormal experiences that often may happen repeatedly in a specific location. They include apparitions, sounds, smells, and the movement and disappearance of objects.

Kahuna – In the Hawaiian tradition, a wise person or Shaman.

Materialization — The visible and/or physical formation by a spirit.

Menehune [pronounced meh—neh—HOO—neh] — Said to be "little people," similar to pixies or trolls, who live in the deep forests and hidden valleys of the Hawaiian Islands, far from the eyes of normal humans.

Orbs — This is the most common type of spirit energy to be captured on film, appearing as solid or transparent "balls". They appear in many shapes and some colors, with white being the most common. Thought to be spirit energy.

Paranormal — Beyond the range of normal experience or scientific explanation.

Parapsychology — The study of the evidence for psychological phenomena, such as telepathy, clairvoyance, and psychokinesis, that are not explainable by science.

Poltergeist — "Noisy Ghost," or "Rumbling Spirit." Manifests as noises, moving objects, fires, marks on the body, and general disorder. Often said to be associated with the release of kinetic or psychokinetic energy of children going through puberty.

Psychometry — The ability to psychically read an object and make associations with someone's life through that object.

Psychokinesis – Moving things with the mind.

Remote Viewing — The practice of seeking impressions about a far away or unseen place, object, or person, using extra-sensory perception.

Residual Haunting — Not technically referred to as a haunting, but more of an energy imprint that manifests as a spirit, and is seen or heard doing the same thing at specific intervals. Perhaps the spirit is trapped repeating a specific moment in life, or this may be perhaps it is just a traumatic flash from the past during a traumatic moment.

Shaman — A highly- trained and spiritually evolved person.

Shamanism — A range of beliefs and practices used to communicate with the spiritual world. Most often used by indigenous peoples.

Spirit — The soul or principle principal force within a living being. The soul. A; also, a supernatural entity.

Spirit Guide — A term used by Spiritualist churches, mediums, and psychics to describe a disincarnate spirit who acts as a guide or protector to a living human being.

Vision Board — A visualization tool used to attract things you want into your life. By studying Using items cut from magazines, drawings, and writings, the theory is that by studying these items, you will be able to become the person you want to become and make your dreams become reality.

About the Author

Karen Zimmerman is a former journalist, and the author of two self-published books – *Ghost Stories of Alameda* and *Ghost Stories of Alameda, Vol. 2*, and of *Ghost Stories and Legends of Alameda, Berkeley and Oakland*, published by Schiffer Publishing in 2010.

She lives in Alameda, Calif.

CPSIA information can be obtained at www.ICGtesting.com
Printed in the USA
LVOW041202170911

246717LV00001BA/173/P

9 781600 763168